Which Wa Ecology Mc ̣ ̣ment?

Essays by
Murray Bookchin

- The Future of the Ecology Movement

- Will Ecology Become "the Dismal Science"?

- The Population Myth

- Sociobiology or Social Ecology?

Library of Congress Cataloguing-in-Publication Data

Bookchin, Murray, 1921-
    Which way for the ecology movement? / essays by Murray Bookchin,
        p.   ca.
    ISBN 1-873176-26-0
    I. Human ecology--Philosophy. 2. Environmentalism. I. Title
    GF21.B6 1993
    304.2--dc20

British Library Cataloguing in Publication Data

Bookchin, Murray
    Which Way for the Ecology Movement?:
    I. Title
    333.7

    ISBN 1-873176-26-0

Library of Congress Catalog Number: 93-074334

First published in 1994 by

AK Press   AK Press
22 Lutton Place   P.O. Box 40682
Edinburgh, Scotland   San Francisco, CA
8HE 9PE   94140-0682

Typeset and design donated by Freddie Baer.

Contents

PREFACE

These essays were written at different times in the past decade for different publications in the United States. Inasmuch as they deal with closely related subjects like Malthusianism, sociobiology, and mystical ecology, they unavoidably repeat certain basic themes that I could not remove without weakening individual essays. The reader will find points in one essay that are dealt with again in another. I ask for forbearance when such repetitions appear.

I wish to thank *The Progressive* for granting me permission to republish the essay, "Will Ecology Become 'the Dismal Science'?" and Janet Biehl, my colleague and companion, for criticizing and editing the introduction. Time has not diminished the issues I have discussed in what follows: if anything, they are as important for the future of the ecology movement as they were in the past.

Murray Bookchin
February 1993

INTRODUCTION:
THE FUTURE OF THE ECOLOGY MOVEMENT

AT THE TIME WHEN I BEGAN TO WRITE about ecological issues in 1951 (my book-length article "The Problem of Chemicals in Food" was published early in 1952), I had begun to view environmentally oriented movements as potentially the most radical that could emerge from the socially deadening 1950s and even the politically convoluted 1960s. Even before the debacle of the New Left, my hopes were already focused on ecologism and feminism; on municipal socialism, as it was called in Britain; on the citizens' initiative movements in Germany; and on confederal municipalism or libertarian municipalism, as I began to call it in 1971 — basically, the development of a grassroots counterpower to the nation-state and parliamentarism.

The ability of modern capitalism to coopt almost everything, however, never ceases to amaze me. Despite all the predictions that the radicals of my 1930s generation had made about capitalism's imminent demise on the eve of the Second World War, capitalism actually emerged from that conflict stronger and more stable than we could have ever imagined. Moreover, it had been radically transformed. To an unprecedented degree, industry had begun to rely on state intervention in order to manage incipient crises; trades unions were substantially integrated into the prevailing social order and were used to blunt labor militancy rather than express it. The workers' movement that I had known in the 1930s ceased to be a viable candidate for the "hegemonic" role that the Anarchosyndicalism and Marxism of the Old Left had assigned to it, despite the sporadic upsurges that occurred in the postwar era. Indeed, the proletariat in the United States came to view itself as patently "middle-class," to the point that nowadays liberal journalists joke about it; and traditional radical parties either melted away or mutated along expressly liberal and middle-class lines.

The New Left, too, after its promising anarchic and populist beginnings, eventually degenerated into the very Trotskyism that I had abandoned in my youth. Nor have the "new social movements" that I regarded as central to any advance in radical politics been spared

1

these mutations. They too are being coopted by modern capitalism. By the eighties, feminism, certainly one of the most antihierarchical and potentially radical movements, had divided into two tendencies: one sought a "fair" place for women within the existing social order — in business, the state machinery, and even the military; the other, a growing minority, drifted toward Goddess worship, wiccan practices, and self-cultivation and actually hypostasized the very traits that patriarchy had long attributed to women — a passive-receptive sensibility, "caring," intuitionism, and antirationalism. The only difference from such patriarchal views of women is that these new feminists consider the cognitive and emotive abilities dubiously attributed to women to be superior to "male" rationality and activism. (On this score, the reader would do well to consult Janet Biehl's *Rethinking Ecofeminist Politics* [Boston: South End Press, 1990].) Had well-organized Anarchist movements emerged that were more receptive to the "new social movements" generally, this drift into capitalist institutions or exotic mystical ideologies might have been averted, or at least significantly challenged.

Ecologism, too, as a political movement of broad implications that essentially centers on humanity's interaction with the natural world, is currently under ideological siege. Yet it still constitutes an important battleground that radical tendencies cannot afford to ignore. The New Age *Zeitgeist* of our time, wherein a personal retreat into the self holds greater sway than social activism, has given rise to mystical, spiritualistic, and ideologically regressive views that purvey a broad array of anticivilizational, antitechnological, and literally antihumanistic nostrums. Many deep ecologists, tapping out condemnations of technology on their word processors (Gary Snyder, the poet laureate of deep ecology, recently devoted a full-page paean to his word processor in *Whole Earth Review*), extol voluntary simplicity, a return to "Paleolithic spirituality," the virtues of hunter-gatherer societies, and the vices of urban living. Not infrequently, they condemn agriculture — even organic agriculture — as a threat to "wilderness." More basically, deep ecology advances "biocentric" notions in opposition to "anthropocentrism" that attribute to human beings equivalent "intrinsic worth" with all other life-forms, including viruses, as in the "Noah principle" that David Ehrenfeld advanced in his *The Arrogance of Humanism* (New York: Oxford University Press, 1981, pp. 207-11). Even the "father of deep ecology," Arne Naess, advances "biospherical egalitarianism" in his typically convoluted, often self-contradictory works.

2

The "biocentrism" ideology of deep ecology and ecomysticism pivots on an ideological trick: a strict assertion of biocentric "rights" is sharply counterposed to an equally strict condemnation of anthropocentric "rights," as though no body of ethical ideas could be formulated that transcended *both* extremes. Yet these extremes can indeed be transcended in an ethics of complementarity, in which human beings — themselves products of natural evolution, with naturally as well as culturally endowed capacities that no other lifeform possesses — can play an actively *creative* role in evolution to the benefit of life generally. Biocentrists willfully ignore such notions — that is, when they do not willfully degrade them into a crude anthropocentrism that they can so easily oppose.

In a natural world from which human beings were absent, no ethics, no concept of "rights," indeed, no notion of "intrinsic worth," could possibly exist. Human beings are required to be able to formulate such "rights" and to extend them to include women, slaves, and the oppressed. Indeed, without a highly conscious and generous humanity, such "rights" could hardly be extended to animals, plants, or by a leap of faith into an intellectual abyss, to the "Cosmos" with all its flaming stars, its black holes, and possibly its extraterrestrial "aliens," whose existence Arne Naess feels we cannot rule out. Nor can the need for the existence of humanity as a unique species be bypassed by rhetoric and half-finished thoughts or clouded over by a mystical haze. That such "biocentric," indeed "cosmocentric" (to coin a word) views have been absorbed to one degree or another by ecomystics, ecotheologians, Goddess disciples, ecoprimitivists, antitechnologists, and even certain ecofeminists has raised serious questions about where the ecology movement is going and the kind of influence it can have.

THIS MYSTICAL ENSEMBLE IS conspicuously asocial in its concerns. Ecological "redemption," as recast in Rudolf Bahro's recent vagaries, tends to take the form of personal "salvation," turning the acolyte inward in a soul-searching pursuit of spirituality and a transpersonal psychologism singularly bereft of social concerns. The understanding that ecological dislocations have their principal sources in social dislocations — the keystone idea of social ecology — is largely displaced by messages of individual self-transformation, as though the two were in contradiction to each other. Deeply dystopian in its denial of all human progress or any prospect thereof, often misanthropic in its antihumanism, distrustful of the so-called "cult of reason" (to use

3

Ehrenfeld's phrase), these very real cults of irrationality and inwardness often explicitly reject social concerns in favor of largely personal attitudes. As one avowed deep ecologist put it in response to my article "Will Ecology Become 'the Dismal Science'?" (in this collection), "Capitalism is not the root cause of our mistreatment of the environment" but rather is "a consequence of our devaluation and alienation from nature." This letter went on to conclude that it is "unacceptable" for social ecologists to attempt to bring ecology into "an already crowded agenda of social issues."

In deep ecology's derogation of the social, the alienation of humans from the natural world (read: *wilderness*) was originally caused by human subjectivity. It is not capitalism, you see, that produced alienation from "Nature," but alienation from "Nature" that produced capitalism. Was this alienation effected by Christianity, as Lynn White, Jr., would have us believe? Or by egotism, as various psychoanalysts would claim? Or was it in fact the same "Paleolithic spirituality" for which deep ecologists yearn, that in fact unavoidably divided the hunter from the hunted, the natural world from the social, and animals from the human beings who manipulated them in animistic religious beliefs? In any case it is our *attitudes* and *psychological makeup* or "mindscapes" that we must explore in this most therapeutic of eras — even at the expense of addressing a "crowded agenda" of social problems that so patently yield ecological problems.

Despite their indifference to social issues and their emphasis on personal "salvation," ecomystics usually premise their views on a biometaphysics, as contradictory as this may seem. Ecofeminist celebrations of the alleged intuitive powers and soulful mystery of women over "male" rationality and aggressiveness easily lend themselves to a crude sociobiologism that is more genetic than cultural. The numinous "self" that we presumably must develop within a Cosmic "Self" if we are to attain "self-realization," to use the language of Arne Naess, Bill Devall, and George Sessions, has very earthy implications that can lead to highly reactionary conclusions.

Ecomystics of one kind or another tend to be in the forefront of what I would call a "hunger politics" that celebrates a Calvinistic material denial, a Taoist quietism, a Buddhist fatalism, and a sociobiological interpretation of human nature. More disconcertingly, these ecomystics are among the most vociferous advocates of neo-Malthusianism, immigration control, a derogatory image of human nature, and a privileging of "wilderness" over human habitats. The

4

emphasis they place on this kind of *political* agenda verges on the misanthropic. With their social crudity, as though an abstract "Humanity" and its attitudes were responsible for ecological problems rather than capitalists and their profit grubbing, ecomystics excel in standing reality on its head instead of fixing it firmly on its feet. For all their talk about "Humanity's" need for a sense of "Oneness" with a vaguely conceived "Nature," they are in fact the most committed of dualists in totally misconceiving the place of human beings in the natural world. Indeed, they project a crude anthropomorphization of biological facts onto the biosphere in the name of a singularly transcendental, Cosmic, and unnatural "Self."

WHICH BRINGS ME TO THE ESSAYS THAT FOLLOW. The subject that unites them is what is indeed a real crisis in outlook that may well determine the future of the ecology movement. While an overview of this crisis is given in "Will Ecology Become 'the Dismal Science'?" originally published in *The Progressive in 1991*, I have concentrated a great deal of my attention in the other essays on the two salient problems that their titles express: "The Population Myth," originally published in two parts in *Green Perspectives* in 1988-89, and "Sociobiology or Social Ecology?" published in two parts in *Harbinger* in 1983-84. ("Sociobiology or Social Ecology?" contains some material from my book *The Ecology of Freedom*, published in 1982, with permission of Chesire Books.) I have not significantly altered these articles. Today, I would use the words "natural world" or "first nature" instead of "nature" for reasons I have explained in the 1991 introduction to my book, *The Ecology of Freedom* (Montreal: Black Rose Books).

The years that have passed since their original publication have not made these essays irrelevant in any sense. Articles on the so-called "overpopulation problem" are now proliferating like mushrooms after a storm in the United States, often in flat ignorance of declining "fertility rates." Sociobiology, for its part, has become sedimented into social theory as well as environmental ideologies as heaven-sent truth. Paul Ehrlich's notorious and hysterically titled 1968 book *The Population Bomb* called for a federal population agency to control demographic growth (this, let me add, was during the Nixon administration). Yet despite the hoopla that surrounded the publication of that book, population growth has been strangely wayward in conforming to Ehrlich's predictions. None of the zany scenarios that Ehrlich or his supporters advanced some twenty-four years ago have come true as of this writing, nor has the "bomb" been as explosive as they predicted. Their various claims that a doubling of the world's population would lead to competition between human beings and insects for the last vestiges of grass on the planet; that the world would run out of petroleum in 1992; that the earth's fertile land would become so limited, and sources of many crucial minerals and metals so exhausted, that agriculture and industry would all but grind to a halt; that habitable areas would become so sparse that artificial islands in the oceans might be needed to provide *Lebensraum* for population overflow around the year 2000 — all of this has turned out to be arrant rubbish.

Not only is extrapolating human population figures as though people were fruit flies, lemmings, or rabbits blatantly fatuous; it abstracts human beings and their proliferation from any cultural context whatever, reducing human numbers to mere biological and statistical facts. Problems of property ownership, economic exploitation, class rule, racial prejudice, gender oppression, nationalism, civil wars between competing repressive rulers, imperialism — *all* are biologized out of existence, presumably in the name of an "ecological thinking" that in fact verges on ecological idiocy. This asocial outlook essentially provides an apologia for the social abuses that lead to ecological ones. I am primarily concerned here with the intellectual, cultural, and spiritual poverty this outlook reflects — and significantly fosters. Despite its popularity among tabloid readers, this approach shares the sheer dumbness that one encounters in deep ecology: its effect is to lower consciousness, not to alert or raise it. Worse still, its conclusions range beyond the specific issues it addresses and feed those simplistic ways of thinking that render people susceptible to manipulative sloganeering and rhetoric, demogagic propaganda, and ideological regression.

IT IS BY USING THIS WAY OF THINKING — interpreting extremely complex problems in highly simplistic ways, reducing qualitative and social problems to vacuous quantitative and biological ones — that Edward Abbey could describe that strange mix of cultures called "American" as "northern European" (read: Aryan?); that David Foreman of the original Earth First! (read: People Second?) could abjure philanthropic individuals from giving aid to starving Ethiopian children so that "Nature" could "take its course"; and that "Miss Ann Thropy" (read: Christopher Manes?) in the pages of the early *Earth First!* journal could welcome the AIDS plague as a means for "controlling" population. To quibble about the viciousness of these utterances (at least one of which was retracted because of the uproar I raised about them) misses the point completely. People may err quite understandably about ideas out of ignorance. But is it not the case that certain views follow *logically* from fairly implicit *premises*? If reasoned consistently, B will follow from A and C will follow from B. So do concepts follow from one another, given the foundations in which they are rooted. Abhorrent as their conclusions are, Abbey, Foreman, and "Miss Ann Thropy" were not "wrong" *if* it is agreed that human beings are "intrinsically" equal in "worth" to fleas, cats, deer, or tuna fish, and hence are subject to unlimited reproduction until starvation and/or epidemic intervenes. Like other creatures whose increasing numbers have destroyed their ecological niches, our remote primate ancestors may indeed have starved in times of food shortages or, for all we know, as a result of excessive reproduction.

But the point is that human beings are *not* subject to "Nature's" blind operations. If they are subject to anything, it is their highly changeable social institutions, relationships, cultural traditions, ideologies, technologies, and the like — what Marx rather ineptly called "social law." They can consciously change their seemingly "natural" destinies decisively, rationally, and willfully — assuming, to be sure, that their brains have not been desiccated by the kind of asocial thinking that enters into neo-Malthusian, deep ecology, and ecomystical ideologies. More generally, they are obliged to explore the *implications* that a given set of premises can yield and decisively reject those that may in fact diminish their claim to be *Homo sapiens* — or rather figuratively, "intelligent people." They have to explore where a given body of ideas *leads* — not accept assertions and calculations at face value simply because they *seem* "deep" and are decorated with ecological rhetoric.

Ecology, in particular, can lend itself to very creative and promising, indeed, richly naturalistic and cooperative conclusions. But as an outlook, not merely as a branch of biology, it can also lead to very sinister social conclusions such as racism, nationalism, and elitism if they are used to justify what the Nazis called *Kultur* or imperialism or very definitely fascism. When an ecomystic like Rudolf Bahro speaks of the "Green Adolf" within us and our need for a "prince of the ecological turn," he is playing with fire. Indeed, biocentrism was extremely fashionable in the Third Reich among Heinrich Himmler's crowd — which did not interfere with his operations as the administrator of death camps like Auschwitz.

At the risk of being provocative, albeit not accusatory, I must point out that nature-mysticism permeated the thinking and avowals of the most murderous of the Nazi leaders. And we cannot ignore how dangerous it can be to flirt with ideas like biocentrism in dealing with social phenomena. It is not accidental that during the Second World War Hitler called his East Prussian headquarters the "Wolf Lair," in accordance with his mystification of an Earth, Folk, and Race ideology. Biocentrism appears in several pages of his *Mein Kampf*, while Himmler declaimed in a notorious letter: "How can you find pleasure in shooting from behind cover at poor creatures browsing on the edge of a wood, innocent, defenseless, and unsuspecting? It's really pure murder. Nature is so marvelously beautiful, and every animal has a right to live." Thereupon this mass murderer proceeded to celebrate "Indo-Germanic" and Buddhist sensitivity to the "rights" of all life-forms, while "with us, every slug is trampled on, every worm destroyed!" (Quoted in Robert A. Pois, "Man in the Natural World: Some Implications of the National Socialist Religion," in *Political Symbolism in Modern Europe*, ed. Seymour Drescher [New Brunswick, N.J.: Transaction Books, 1982].) That young *Wandervögel*, members of a romantic "nature" youth movement early in this century that celebrated freedom from civilization and closeness to the earth, drifted in large numbers into the Nazi movement should warn us that "reverence for Nature" may often exclude respect for human beings — and that it is fraught with dangerous as well as benign "implications" (to use Pois's word).

Clearly, I am not saying here that a liberal like Arne Naess, a transpersonal ecologist like Warwick Fox, a genial mystic like Satish Kumar, or even a basically social democratic "demographer" like Paul Ehrlich — all of whom are deep ecologists in some sense or other — are National Socialists. But what are we to say of figures like Herbert Gruhl, a far-right-wing German ecologist? Or Rudolf Bahro, whose recent ideas overlap greatly with deep ecology? Or Edward Abbey, whose writings can easily be interpreted as ecofascistic? It has been remarkably easy for French workers, including many who were formerly Communists in Paris's famous "Red Belt," to shift over to the quasi-fascistic National Front of Jean-Marie Le Pen, and for youthful Communists in the former East Germany to become skinheads after unification. What I am arguing for is the need *to closely examine the premises of one's views,* and the ways they could *potentially* unfold if they are not critically examined and subjected to rational evaluation.

THIS PROBLEM BECOMES all the more urgent when *rationality* itself is denigrated and *intuitive* vagaries are hypostasized. Or when *personal* introspection is valued over the "crowded social agenda" of these troubled times. Or when neopaganism, Goddess worship, and a "Paleolithic" or "Neolithic" sensibility (whatever these may have been) are celebrated, while the idea of human progress is despised as mythic, and advocacy of human intervention into the natural world — *irrespective of the kind of society in which it occurs or the goals it is meant to achieve* — evokes frowns at best and condemnation at worst? That a deep ecologist like Robyn Eckersley can call Walter Truett Anderson's demand that people "govern evolution" an example of "ecological restoration," and then go on to denigrate permaculture — a nearly passive-receptive technique for cultivating food — as interventionist, is patently inconsistent. Her outright incongruities can only be dismissed as absurd.

Nor can we mystify preindustrial, even aboriginal, lifeways by rewriting anthropology, archaeology, and history to suit a preconceived, uncritical image of the past along mystical ecology's biased lines. Much as the admirable features in the various native American cultures, for example, deserve celebration, the vast mosaic of pre-Columbian societies cannot be overgeneralized as a single "culture" with a single "primal mind." The Aztec culture was heavily anchored in human sacrifice and conquest; the woodland Iroquois tribes warred with each other continually, until they were brought together into a confederacy, after which the alliance itself became highly predatory in relationship to many of its Algonkian neighbors. The remote Yuqui Indians of South America practiced hereditary slavery in the Amazon despite a deculturation that left with them with little more of a technology than longbows and boar-tooth scrapers. Egalitarian as some presumably "Pleistocene," "Neolithic," or "Mesolithic" communities were *internally*, it is no exaggeration to say that they often lived in chronic hostility to "outside" tribes and villages. We may agree that civilization has been, as Hegel put it, a "slaughterbench," yet its achievements, including its relatively free urban life that made possible the intermingling of strangers, has the *potential* to replace tribal folk parochialism with a new ideal of a universal humanity.

Rewriting anthropology and history to support claims for the superiority of the precivilizational past without recognizing that humanity must go beyond *both* past and present to integrate their achievements and abandon their failings, paradoxically fosters an

9

inward acquiescence to the *present* and to a belief in the eternality of the status quo. Clearly, no return to precivilization is possible. Nor can "wilderness" be recovered, even in the form of theme parks, without human protection and hence human intervention. Indeed, to return to primally "simple means," as quite a number of ecomystics would have us do in principle (rarely, to be sure, in practice, in an era of word processors and other electronic devices), would involve a technological regression so sweeping that the freedom from toil so necessary for a participatory democracy and a sensitivity to the natural world would vitiate the "rich ends" that we all aspire to achieve. A technologically primitive society would be embroiled in a struggle for minimal material privileges and would thus exacerbate class exploitation. The data on which Marshall Sahlins based his notion of the "original affluent society" — particularly Richard Lee's findings on the caloric intake and health of Kalahari desert foragers — is now known to be erroneous, as recent critiques of Lee's findings suggest. Kalahari aborigines knew hunger, misery, malnutrition, and early death — all myths about the "affluent" lives of "noble savages" to the contrary notwithstanding.

Yet if we neither should nor can return to the past, can we remain in the irrational present? Can we use the balms of therapy and introspection and cultivate of a "self" that is part of a cosmic "Self" to rectify the ecological crisis that faces us? My contention as a social ecologist is that we cannot; indeed, that we must *press further, beyond past and present,* to a new society and sensibility that challenges the irrationalities of our time and seeks out the basic, eminently social causes that produce them.

THE PREMISES OF ECOMYSTICISM may lead in many directions, but a goal of social freedom seems to be surprisingly rarely expressed in the literature. Indeed, deep ecology and ecomysticism generally would be reactionary and alienating if the logic of their precepts were actually carried out in practice. The logic of a seemingly benign deep ecology demand for "biocentric egalitarianism" involves the surrender of human freedom to "Nature's" imperatives. If sociobiology predetermines a great deal of "human nature" in what E. O. Wilson calls "the morality of the gene," deep ecology, in turn, seems to place social life into subordination — and a very real subordination — to the "hunger politics" of "voluntary simplicity" and outright asceticism. The logic of permitting "Nature" to "take its course" (as David Foreman once put it) is to render human beings no different in their "intrinsic worth" from other animals and hence subject to "natural laws" like unrelenting swings in population numbers. The tendency of deep ecology ideologists to stop halfway in thinking out the implications of their premises is matched only by their failure to "deeply" confront real social problems and their impact on the natural world.

Logically, biocentrism's precept that *life* should not be taken except to meet an organism's "vital needs" — presumably, its need to survive — should lead its supporters to oppose abortion and, lacking any serious emphasis on human freedom, to accept a "right-to-life" position. If every life-form has an *equal* right to flourish, then women's right to abortion and hence to reproductive freedom should be dismissed as "anthropocentric." A human fetus is no less "alive" than a microbe, a flea, or a grizzly bear. Deep ecologists and ecomystics may well agree with the pro-choice movement that the real question surrounding abortion is not "life" as such (actually, the *pivotal* idea of biocentrism) but whether a fetus constitutes a human being. But if the "right" of a fetus to "self-realization" is to be weighed against the arguable "needs" of its potential mother, whose own survival does not necessarily depend upon whether the fetus is permitted to develop, then logic forces us to support the *biological* "right" of the fetus over the social, ethical, and political rights of women to choose whether to have children. In general, if we are to be guided by a consistent biocentric outlook, then we should forgo social rights that contradict biological "rights," since a body of biological "rights" based on "intrinsic worth" supersedes any body of social rights based on freedom, much as sociobiological attempts to recast human behavior largely in terms of a "morality of the gene" tend to outweigh, indeed supplant cultural factors in influencing behavior.

Yet abortion rights patently affect rates of population growth, which ecomystics of all kinds have also made into a major issue, and as such they are required fully to support women's rights to abortion. Thus, neo-Malthusian attempts to reduce social facts to biological facts divide into pro-choice demands for reproductive freedom and anti-abortionist claims to the rights of the unborn. The abortion issue, in fact, points up the absurd tangle of contradictions — partly in theory, partly in practice — which biocentrism produces and the extent to which it remains a thoroughly unthought-out, one-sided, and irrational outlook.

Granted we must deal kindly — and for many individuals, lovingly — with nonhuman life-forms. Granted too that wilderness, insofar as this term has meaning nowadays when the biosphere has been irrevocably altered by human action, should be protected, even expanded, and that the integrity of the natural world should be a matter of profound concern. Yet let us not forget that wilderness preservation is an eminently *social* issue, and its future depends profoundly upon the type of social system as well as the values we develop. Cruelty to human beings, let me add, often goes hand in hand with a neglect of nonhuman life-forms and wild areas, despite Edward Abbey's statement in *Desert Solitaire* (page 20) that he would rather kill a man than a snake.

This much can be said with certainty: a sensitivity to life and to the tribulations that all life-forms endure depends upon the development of human culture and sensitivity. Not surprisingly, a love of the natural world has been cultivated mainly by city dwellers and people educated in an urban milieu — be they Thoreau, Tolstoy, or Carson — who have developed a cultural sensitivity for the natural world and particularly for nonhuman animals. Curiously, this is often less true of many foragers, like the Mbuti pygmies, for example, whose cruelty to wildlife Colin Turnbull clearly documented in his highly sympathetic account of their lifeways.

The ways in which we interact with each other as social beings profoundly influence attitudes we are likely to have toward the natural world. Any sound ecological perspective rests in great part on our social perspectives and interrelationships; hence, to draw up an ecological agenda that has no room for social concerns is as obtuse as to draw up a social agenda that has no room for ecological concerns. Indeed, any attempt to distinguish one from the other, or to focus on one at the expense of the other, can and has led to an outright lack of concern for the ways animals we call human treat one another — and concomitantly, to an ugly misanthropic outlook.

There is indeed a great deal to concern us about a biocentric outlook, just as there is about an anthropocentric outlook. The various forms of antihumanism that are advanced today go well beyond these allegedly biocentric implications. There can be little doubt that Haitian refugees have been denied entry into the United States, or gypsies deported from Germany, for of racist reasons, not merely the economic reasons adduced by the American and German governments. The burgeoning nationalism, xenophobia, parochialism, and tribalism that have claimed an inestimable number of lives in recent times cannot be attributed to Malthusian myths that blame wars and conflicts on overpopulation or a dwindling food supply. These ills patently have their roots in traditional folk hatreds, civil conflicts between clan leaders, local imperialistic interests, and international meddling that reaches back to the armaments that the United States and the Soviet Union supplied to "Third World" nations and movements that they regarded as strategically important in the Cold War.

Invoking biologistic causes for the world's abundant conflicts and dislocations creates an apologistic patina for these profoundly social problems. Neo-Malthusians invoke "overpopulation," deep ecologists invoke "anthropocentrism," ecotheologians invoke "avarice," ecofeminists invoke "male aggressiveness," ecomystics generally invoke "rationality," Jungians appeal to immutable archetypes, Freudians cite stages of human development — and inevitably, sociobiologists invoke intractable, even "selfish genes." What these modern, largely mystical attributions share is that they all regard social dislocations as the result of a biologically determined "human nature" — and only rarely, if ever, of social forces like capitalism, hierarchy, the market imperative of "grow or die," or corporate balance-sheets. That human beings are far from constituting a unified "humanity" — divided as they are by gender, ethnicity, nationality, skin color, status, wealth, and vocational privileges, in short, hierarchy and class, oppressed and oppressor, exploiter and exploited — tends to be swept under the carpet.

CONTRARY TO WHAT MY MYSTICAL AND DEEP ECOLOGY CRITICS so dishonestly claim, I am not at all indifferent to *spirituality*. I am a naturalist in my thinking who has an admitted aversion to *spiritualism*, which is what so many of them propound, with its often mystical leanings at best and outright religiosity at worst. In many books, articles, and lectures I have repeatedly propounded the need for a new sensibility, character structure, ethics, and nonhierarchical view of the nonhuman as well as human worlds.

Still further, with a persistence, if not an ignorance, that verges on the demagogic, the mystical and deep ecology crowd invariably misrepresent my views as a continuation of the Old Left's economistic or political dogmas, often on the basis of an article in which I criticized Foreman's hunger politics and "Miss Ann Thropy's" accolades for the AIDS epidemic. Some of these critics, I may add, lavishly praised, cited, and quoted from my works before I began to criticize their own pet panaceas. Nor have they always exhibited very much polemical

13

gentility of their own. They have consistently distorted my views; they have flung galling accusations at me as being a supporter of homophobic and other reactionary causes; and they have accused me of having a technocratic mentality, despite my pioneering work in the early 1960s in support of wind and solar power, organic agriculture, and ecologically oriented technologies. Ecomystics and deep ecology acolytes are to be particularly reproved for characterizing my concerns for "social justice" as "anthropocentric" — an almost routine response to my criticisms of their views — with a fatuity that reveals how little they know of my works and the cynicism with which they distort my views.

It may be well possible to coopt many of the demands that the "new social movements" make by enlarging the presence of women in the state and on corporate boards, by opening commanding positions for them in the military, and by rearing Mother Earth Goddess shrines — even by creating public spaces for Starhawk to engage in wiccan rituals. It may also be possible to create new "grassroots" school boards and hold staged "town meetings" and local "city halls" in the name of decentralization and a polished, well-functioning "participatory democracy." Even "workers' control" is coming into fashion in the corporate world, as witness the growing extent to which firms bring workers into decision-making processes, hiring and firing, and of course, the formulation of production quotas — that is to say, into complicity with their own exploitation. The potential radicalism of a movement emerging from deeply felt social and ecological concerns can easily be smothered by an ideological array of transpersonal, mystical, and Jungian approaches for personal "self-realization," an almost Calvinistic emphasis on "simple living," and a Taoist belief in "going with the flow."

The more intelligent bourgeoisie know they have nothing to fear from such nostrums. Property ownership, economic growth, profit increases, "healthy competition," and "free enterprise" will continue along quite merrily regardless. In the meantime, capitalism will insidiously simplify the biosphere (making due allowances for "wilderness" reserves and theme parks), steadily reduce the organic to the inorganic and the complex to the simple, and convert soil into sand — all at the expense of the biosphere's integrity and viability. The state will still be an ever-present means for keeping oppressed people at bay and will "manage" whatever crises emerge as best it can. Ultimately, society will tend to become more and more authoritarian, public life will atrophy, and subjectivism and egotism will erode the

14

remaining vestiges of a radical politics and social commitment — all in the name of achieving "self-realization."

Can anyone who reflects on the realities of a society premised on growth seriously believe that if the world's population were reduced to half or even to a tenth of what it is today, the market economy would actually reduce its output of goods? That the market competition that drives the present economy would come to a halt? That growth and ecological devastation would cease? That the vast media apparatus that fosters consumerism would disappear? That "new markets" would not be "developed," to use corporate argot, by encouraging people to buy what they do not need, or by increasing armaments sales at home and/or abroad, or by restarting a cold or hot war to "create new jobs" — and new cemeteries? Here the social naivete of the population bombers, ecomystics, and deep ecologists reveals itself with a vengeance. And there will be more than enough sociobiologists around to justify "our" anti-ecological behavior, aggressiveness, greed, and perhaps patriarchy by locating them in the "morality of the gene." This unsavory combination of ecomysticism, Malthusianism, and sociobiology in all their various mutations that reduces our social ills to biologistic and personalistic causes is a sure-fire ideological resource for modern elites. Arguing that birth rates and genes determine our behavior gives biological facts priority over the corporate interests and state institutions that are so obviously implicated in the ecological and social ills that afflict the world today. The "self" then becomes the introverted battleground for "resolving" the social crises that have been growing over the years and that threaten to become planetary explosions in the decades to come.

Does a focus on the social and political arenas, in turn, mean that we must postpone giving our attention to or organizing against the immediate environmental abuses that afflict us today, until fundamental changes have been made in society? Arne Naess's assertion that I hold this bizarre view has been echoed in various formulations by at least two of deep ecology's most prominent theorists, Warwick Fox and George Sessions, then repeated by many of deep ecology's lesser lights as gospel truth. In flat refutation of this canard, I will cite only one of several explicit examples to the contrary in my works. As early as 1969, some three years before Naess coined the words "deep ecology," I wrote a manifesto for Ecology Action East (no longer in existence) under the title "The Power to Create, the Power to Destroy," in which I declared: "Ecology Action East supports every effort to conserve the environment: to eliminate nuclear power plants and weapons, to preserve clean air and water, to limit the use of pesticides and food additives, to reduce vehicular traffic on streets and highways, to make cities more wholesome physically, to prevent radioactive wastes from seeping into the environment, to guard and expand wilderness areas and domains for wildlife, to defend animal species from human depredation." Let me emphasize that this clear and unqualified call to action on *every kind of environmental problem that we face* included an appeal to guard and expand wilderness areas and wildlife habitats, and to oppose cruelty to animals. What the manifesto clearly voiced at the same time was a *warning* — one that is so often muted or dealt with in naively social and reformist statements — that such "delaying actions" are not a substitute for "a definitive solution to the fundamental conflict that exists between the present social order and the natural world," nor can they "arrest the overwhelming momentum of the existing society for destruction." (This manifesto, "The Power to Create, The Power to Destroy," is included in my essay collection *Toward an Ecological Society*, Montreal: Black Rose Books, 1980, pp. 43-44. Since this edition of the manifesto contains later, additional material on organization, the date is given as November 1979 instead of 1969.)

What makes it ultimately impossible for modern capitalism to coopt ecologism as it has other "new social movements" is that two irreconcilable imperatives are in collision with each other: the "grow-or-die" imperatives that drive the capitalist economy toward ever-greater expansion or growth, with all its consequences for the environment, and the complex ecological factors on which the integrity of the biosphere depends. This collision, with all its dire consequences for life on the planet, will continue to occur as long as the present society exists, irrespective of the sensibilities, ideologies, personal behavior, or Pollyanna views held by a relatively privileged fraction of the Euro-American world.

Identifying the natural world as "wilderness" or as a transcendental "Cosmos," as deep ecologists, ecomystics, and the like generally do, does more than cloak dire social imperatives with a mystical pseudo-reality. It actually intensifies our alienation from the natural world, despite the fact that many deep ecology acolytes regard this very alienation as the source of our social problems. Consider George Sessions, for one, who deprecates subsistence agriculture, since it "destroys tropical forests" — as though ordinary farming families could cultivate food without cutting down trees to one degree or another; consider, even more absurdly, Robyn Eckersley, who opposed permaculture in her critique of my views.

Underlying various qualifiers, contortions of syntax, and equivocal formulations, ecomystics in their many incarnations look askance at all human activity beyond foraging at best or deprecate it at worst, in favor of a mythic realm of wilderness — such that even subsistence farming is frowned upon as harmful to their highly mystified natural world. In view of this we are obliged to ask what contact with reality this very privileged middle-class segment of Euro-American society offers to peasant peoples in the "Third World." By what right do these privileged individuals write paeans to wilderness on their word processors, or use highly complex implements like binoculars to rapturously marvel at the acrobatics of dolphins, or employ sophisticated cameras to capture the sweeping flight of birds — and then go on to sermonize, as George Sessions does, from his ideological fastness that the hungry of the "Third World" would be wiser, perhaps, to establish shantytowns around mega-cities than clear forested areas to fill their bellies and those of their children? Are agribusiness, loggers, mining companies, and ranchers less complicitous in the destruction of forests than farmers and peasants? And what could do more to intensify human alienation from "nature" than to exclude people from so-called "wilderness" areas, as though people did not belong in the natural world and were not products of natural evolution?

THE ESSAYS THAT FOLLOW emphasize that ecological degradation is, in great part, a product of the degradation of human beings by hunger, material insecurity, class rule, hierarchical domination, patriarchy, ethnic discrimination, and competition. Their focus, in short, is on the inseparability of social problems from ecological problems; hence my use of the name *social ecology*. They attempt to demystify mystical and deep ecology, neo-Malthusianism, and sociobiology, all of which serve to derail serious social critique and orient it toward celebrations of "wilderness," the worship of nature deities, primitivism, often a hatred of technology and science as such, and a denigration of reason and the belief that progress is *possible* — especially progress cast in humanistic or human terms.

It would be a simplification of misanthropy, in my view, simply to define it as a deprecation or hatred of humanity. It is also a deprecation of human *potentialities*, of the *capacity* of the human mind and spirit to

17

reach beyond the given reality and conceive — indeed, strive for — a social and ecological dispensation that is creative and cooperative, ethical and visionary. The misanthropic denial of these human potentialities, which permeates mystical and deep ecology, removes the very heart from any truly radical movement. Aside from its tendency to alienate human beings from the natural world, presumably by frowning upon human intervention into it, it is suffused with an implicit and sometimes explicit pessimism about humanity's very presence on the planet, and by an elitism implicit in the claims of the lonely "mountaineer" and the mythical American soloist — and Indian-killer — for whom a "wilderness" bereft of human life is a playground in which to play the role of a mythic "wild man," often with an eminently industrialized civilization as his foundation. Indeed, there is a curious consumerist streak in those usually white males who "abandon" themselves to the "wild," fitted out with costly knapsacks, bedrolls, binoculars, canteens, compasses, chic boots, campy clothing, and in many cases, book contracts from publishers in the "civilized" world to disseminate their anticivilizational ruminations to a breathless public. None of this would be terribly objectionable as such, apart from its egoistic individualism and message of inward withdrawal, if it were not an ideological means to ignore the irrationalities that mark the present social order.

Moreover, much of the "overpopulation" literature has a remarkable disdain for the truth. We do *not* know if the world's population is "too large." In the United States, the latest fertility rate (1992) is two children per woman, which would lead to an absolute decline in the total population were it not for immigration. And in the United States, as far as I am concerned, immigrants are to be welcomed, not restricted from entering a country that is badly in need of cultural diversity. In Europe, where African, Vietnamese, and other "Third World" immigrants are generally demeaned, obstructions to immigration have not dampened the savage brutality of Euro-American imperialists who continue to plunder the "South's" resources and despoil its cultures such that native populations live in virtual or actual famine conditions. As my Parisian friend Daniel Blanchard exclaimed in horror, "Imagine a France occupied only by Frenchmen!" I would say the same for an America inhabited only by Euro-Americans.

Contrary to neo-Malthusian myths of a geometric increase in population and an arithmetic increase in food resources, nearly the entire world has witnessed a vast increase in foodstuffs, while fertility

18

rates have been declining in many presumably overcrowded countries. India's fertility rates dropped from 5.3 in 1980 to 3.9 in 1991; Indonesia's, from 4.6 to 3; the Philippines', from 5.0 to 4.1; Egypt's, from 6 to 4.4. In Brazil, zero population growth is already a reality. The Malthusian documentaries that show crowds of humans in shantytowns around "Third World" cities seldom emphasize that such cities are teeming because agribusiness, warfare, or civil conflicts between petty chieftains (many of whom, as I noted, were armed by the United States and Russia during the Cold War era) displaced peasants and pastoral peoples from the countryside. Nor can warfare alone account for all famine-stricken areas in Africa. American-controlled financial agencies like the World Bank and the International Monetary Fund have dictated shifts in agriculture from foodstuffs to crops for the international market, policies that have gravely impoverished the food resources available for local sustenance.

In citing these population statistics and changes in rural life, I am not advocating the desirability of population growth as such. Much of the dramatic reduction in birth rates in Europe and the United States has been the result not of paeans to a mystified "wilderness" but of the *freedom* that women have acquired over recent decades to transcend the role that patriarchy assigned to them as mere reproductive factories. Radicals can point with pride to the fact that rising living standards have given greater security to smaller families whose members are in a better position to be concerned with the quality of their lives than traditionally large families in which parents are obliged to raise children for labor and to support themselves in their later years. Science can point with pride to the fact that it has produced medical techniques — and yes, even chemical agents — to practice birth control, not merely nuclear weapons; technology can point with pride to innovations that have removed much domestic drudgery from the lives of women, to which they were confined for so much of history, and diminished the amount of labor necessary to gain the means of life.

That such gains have been terribly tainted by the irrationalities of civilization, particularly capitalism, with its highly systematized exploitation of labor in factories and offices, its devastating wars, its ethnic and national hatreds, and its impoverished everyday life, is no argument against civilization, science, technology, or reason *as such*. Rather, the irrationalities of civilization point up the decivilizing, irrationalizing, and spiritually degrading effects of *hierarchical* societies that have structured all of our thinking and behavior around a

19

mentality of domination and social relations based on the exploitation and debasement of human by human. An ecologism that locates these irrationalities in the human condition as the results of population growth, psychologically fossilized Jungian archetypes, "moralities" of the gene, and deities who are "naturalistic" only by virtue of the double-talk of modern mystical rhetoric — such an ecologism plays directly into the hands of the prevailing anti-ecological social order and its needs. Far from opening our eyes to the sources of present-day environmental problems and bringing the clear light of a naturalistic perspective to their resolution, the biologistic mentality that underpins ecomystics, deep ecologists, population bombers, and sociobiologists pushes us back to the realm of the archaic, to ignorance and superstition, and/or to simplistic recipes that extol the past rather than pave the way to a rational and truly ecological future.

Murray Bookchin
Burlington, Vermont
February 21, 1993

Institute for Social Ecology
Plainfield, Vermont 05667

WILL ECOLOGY BECOME "THE DISMAL SCIENCE?"

ALMOST A CENTURY AND A HALF AGO, Thomas Carlyle described economics as "the dismal science." The phrase was to stick, especially as it applied to economics premised on a supposedly unavoidable conflict between "insatiable needs" and "scarce natural resources." In this economics, the limited bounty provided by a supposedly "stingy nature" doomed humanity to economic slumps, misery, civil strife, and hunger.

Today, the phrase "dismal science" appropriately describes certain trends in the ecology movement — trends that seem to be riding on an overwhelming tide of religious revivalism and mysticism. I refer not to the large number of highly motivated, well-intentioned, and often radical environmentalists who are making earnest efforts to arrest the ecological crisis, but rather to exotic tendencies that espouse deep ecology, biocentrism, Gaian consciousness, and eco-theology, to cite the main cults that celebrate a quasi-religious "reverence" for "Nature" with what is often a simultaneous denigration of human beings and their traits.

Mystical ecologists, like many of today's religious revivalists, view reason with suspicion and emphasize the importance of irrational and intuitive approaches to ecological issues. For the Reverend Thomas Berry, whom many regard as the foremost eco-theologian of our day, the "very rational process that we exalt as the only true way to understanding is by a certain irony discovered to be itself a mythic imaginative dream experience. The difficulty of our times is our inability to awaken out of this cultural pathology."

One does not have to be a member of the clergy to utter such atavistic notions. In a more secular vein, Bill Devall and George Sessions, professors of sociology and philosophy, respectively, who wrote *Deep Ecology,* one of the most widely read books in mystical ecology, offer a message of "self-realization" through an immersion of the personal self in a hazy "Cosmic Self," or, as they put it, a "'self-in-Self' where 'Self' stands for organic wholeness."

The language of *Deep Ecology is* distinctly salvational: "This process of the full unfolding of the self can also be summarized in the

21

phrase: 'No one is saved until we are all saved,' where the phrase 'one' includes not only me, an individual human, but all humans, whales, grizzly bears, whole rain-forest ecosystems mountains and rivers, the tiniest microbes in the soil, and so on." The words "and so on" omit the need to deal with pathogenic microbes, animal vectors of lethal diseases, earthquakes, and typhoons, to cite less aesthetically satisfying beings and phenomena than whales, grizzly bears wolves, and mountains. This selective view of "Mother Nature's" biotic and physiographic inventory has raised some stormy problems for mystical ecology's message of universal salvation.

Mystical ecologists tend to downgrade social issues by reducing human problems (a generally distasteful subject to them) to a "species" level — to matters of genetics. In the words of Pastor Berry, humanity must be "reinvented on the species level" by going "beyond our cultural coding, to our genetic coding, to ask for guidance." The rhetoric that follows this passage in *The Dream of the Earth* verges on the mythopoeic, in which our "genetic coding" binds us "with the larger dimensions of the universe" — a universe that "carries the deep mysteries of our existence within itself." Berry's exhortations enjoy great popularity these days, and have been quoted with approval even in the conventional environmental literature, not to speak of the mystical variety.

Such cosmological evangelism, clothed in ecological verbiage, deprecates humanity. When human beings are woven into the "web of life" as nothing more than one of "Mother Nature's" innumerable species, they lose their unique place in natural evolution as rational creatures of potentially unsurpassed qualities, endowed with a deeply social nature, creativity, and the capacity to function as moral agents.

Anthropocentrism, the quasi-theological notion that the world exists for human use, is derided by mystical ecologists in favor of the equally quasi-theological notion of biocentricity, namely, that all life-forms are morally interchangeable with one another in terms of their "intrinsic worth." In their maudlin *Gaia Meditations*, two mystical ecologists, John Seed and Joanna Macy, enjoin us human mortals to "think to your next death. Will your flesh and bones back into the cycle. Surrender. Love the plump worms you will become. Launder your weary being through the fountain of life." In the mystically overbaked world of the American Sunbelt, such drivel tends to descend to the level of bumper-sticker slogans or is evoked in poetic recitations at various ashrams in Anglo-American cities and towns.

Taken as a whole, the crude reduction of the ecological crisis to biological and psychological sources has produced an equally reductionist body of "correctives" that makes the dismal economics of an earlier time seem almost optimistic by comparison. For many, perhaps most, mystical ecologists, the standard recipe for a "sustainable" future involves a lifestyle based on harsh austerity—basically, a rustic discipline marked by dietary simplicity, hard work, the use of "natural resources" only to meet survival needs and a theistic primitivism that draws its inspiration from an alledged Pleistocene or Neolithic "spirituality" rather than from Renaissance or Enlightenment rationality.

Spirituality and rationality, which mystical ecologies invariably perceive in crassly reductionist and simplistic terms, are pitted against each other as angels and demons. The mystics usually regard technology, science, and reason as the basic sources of the ecological crisis and contend these should be contained or even replaced by toil, divination, and intuition. What is even more troubling is that many mystical ecologists are neo-Malthusians, whose more rambunctious elements regard famine and disease as necessary and even desirable to reduce human population.

THE GRIM FUTURE EVOKED BY MYSTICAL ECOLOGISTS is by no means characteristic of the vision the ecology movement projected a generation ago. To the contrary, radical ecologists of the 1960s celebrated the prospect of a satisfying life, freed from material insecurity, toil and the self-denial produced by the market and bureaucratic capitalism.

This utopian vision, advanced primarily by social ecology in 1964 and 1965, was not antitechnological, antirational or antiscientific. It expressed for the first time in the emerging ecology movement the prospect of a new social, technological, and spiritual dispensation. Social ecology claimed that the idea of dominating nature stemmed from the domination of human by human, in the form not only of class exploitation but of hierarchical domination. Capitalism — not technology, reason, or science as such — produced an economy that was systemically anti-ecological. Guided by the competitive marketplace maxim "grow or die," it would literally devour the biosphere, turning forests into lumber and soil into sand.

Accordingly, the key to resolving the ecological crisis was not only a change in spirituality—and not a regression to prehistoric religiosity — but a sweeping change in society. Social ecology offered the vision of a nonhierarchical, communitarian society that would be based on directly democratic confederal communities with technologies structured around solar, wind, and renewable sources of energy; food cultivation by organic methods; and a combined use of crafts and highly versatile, automatic, and sophisticated machinery to reduce human toil and free people to develop themselves as fully informed and creative citizens.

The disappearance of the utopian 1960s into the reactionary 1970s saw a steady retreat by millions of people into a spiritualistic inwardness that had already been latent in the counterculture of the previous decade. As possibilities for social change began to wane, people sought a surrogate reality to veil the ills of the prevailing society and the difficulty of removing them. Apart from a brief interlude of environmental resistance to the construction of nuclear power plants, large parts of the ecology movement began to withdraw from social concerns to spiritual ones, many of which were crassly mystical and theistic.

In the universities, Lynn White, Jr., whose advocacy of religious explanations for the ecological crisis began to give it an otherworldly character, initiated this withdrawal. Around the same time, Garrett Hardin's *Tragedy of the Commons* brought Malthus's ghost into ecological discourse in the academy, further deflecting the social thrust of the 1960s ecology movement into a demographic numbers game. Both of these academicians had advanced their views largely in *Science* magazine, which has only limited public outreach, so it fell to a California entomologist, Paul Ehrlich, to divert the ecological concerns of the early 1970s from the social domain to the single issue of population growth in a hysterical paperback, *The Population Bomb*, that went through numerous editions and reached millions of readers.

Writing like an SS officer touring the Warsaw ghetto, Ehrlich in the opening pages of his tract saw nothing but "People! People!" —failing to notice a vicious society that had degraded human lives. The slender thread that united White and, more firmly, Hardin and Ehrlich was the nonsocial interpretation they gave to ecological problems, not any shared ecological overview.

Arne Naess, a Norwegian academic and mountain-climber, provided such an overview in 1973. He coined the term "deep ecology" and nurtured it as an ecological philosophy or sensibility that asks "deep questions" in contrast to "shallow ecology." Recycled into a form of California spiritualism by Devall and Sessions with a bizarre mix of Buddhism, Taoism, Native American beliefs, Heidegger, and

24

Spinoza, among others, mystical ecology was now ready to take off as a new "Earth Wisdom."

What catapulted this confused sensibility from the campus into newspaper headlines, however, was a wilderness movement, Earth First!, that began to take dramatic direct actions against the lumbering of old-growth forests and similar indecencies inflicted on wild areas by corporate America.

Earth First!'s founders, particularly David Foreman, had been conservationists who were weary of the ineffectual lobbying tactics of Washington-based conservation organizations. Inspired by Edward Abbey, the author of the highly popular novel *The Monkey Wrench Gang*, whose avowedly misanthropic views bordered on racism with its accolades to America's "northern European culture," Earth First!'s leaders began to seize upon deep ecology as a philosophy.

This is not to say that most Earth First!ers knew anything about "deep ecology" other than its claim to be "deep." But Devall and Sessions had placed Malthus in its pantheon of prophets and described "industrial society" — not capitalism — as the embodiment of the ills that mystical ecologists generally deride. Indeed, their book was distinctly wilderness-oriented, expressly "biocentric," and seemed to make short shrift of humanity's place in the cosmos.

Consistency has never been the strong point of any antirational movement, so it is not surprising that while Devall and Sessions piously extolled a "self-in-Self," a caring form of pantheism or hylozoism, Foreman did not hesitate to describe human beings as a "cancer" in the natural world, and quite surprisingly, Gary Snyder, the poet-laureate of the deep ecology movement, described humans as "locust-like."

MYSTICAL ECOLOGY AS A DISMAL SCIENCE IS, in fact, antihuman. Despite his gentle piety, Pastor Berry, for example, becomes positively ferocious in his treatment of human beings, describing them as "the most pernicious mode of earthly being." Indeed, "We are the termination, not the fulfillment, of the Earth process. If there were a parliament of creatures, its first decision might well be to vote the humans out of the community, too deadly a presence to tolerate any further. We are an affliction of the world, its demonic presence. We are the violation of Earth's most sacred aspects."

Clerical vitriol has often been more selective. In the best of cases, it has targeted the rich, not the poor; the oppressor, not the oppressed; the ruler, not the downtrodden. But mystical ecology tends to be more all-embracing. Berry's ecumenical "we," like his treatment of "human beings" as a species rather than as beings who are divided by the oppressions of race, sex, material means of life, culture, and the like, tends to permeate mystical ecology.

"We are all capitalists at heart," declares a well-intentioned Norwegian writer, Erik Dammann, whose *The Future in Our Hands* has been touted by Arne Naess as a virtual manifesto for social improvement. The homeless in American cities, the AIDS victims who have been left to die in Zurich's notorious needle park, the overworked people in the First World's mines and factories — none of these count for much in Dammann's plea that "we" in America and Europe reduce our consumption of goods in behalf of the Third World's poor.

Laudable as the goal of reduced consumption may seem, it is an ineffectual exercise in charity, not social mobilization; in humanitarianism, not social change. It is also an exercise in a superficial form of social analysis that grossly underplays the profoundly systemic factors that have produced overfed elites in all parts of the world and masses of underfed underlings. Nearly all we learn from Dammann's liberal good intentions is that an ecumenical "we" must be faulted for the ills of the world — a mystical "consumer" who greedily demands goodies that "our" overworked corporations are compelled to produce.

Despite the radical rhetoric to which Devall and Sessions resort, the principal *practical* recipe for social change they have to offer "us" in *Deep Ecology* is little more than a naive prayer. "Our first principle," they write, "is to encourage agencies, legislators, property owners and managers to consider flowing with rather than forcing natural processes." We should "act through the political process to inform managers and government agencies of the principles of deep ecology," to achieve "some significant changes in the direction of wise long-range management policies."

The watered-down liberalism of Devall and Sessions is echoed more explicitly in Paul and Anne Ehrlich's latest book, *Healing the Planet*, in which the authors declare their adherence to deep ecology, a "quasi-religious movement" (to use their own words) that "recognizes that a successful new philosophy cannot be based on scientific nonsense." Such denigration of science hardly befits writers whose reputation is based on their scientific credentials, with or without the vague use of the word "nonsense" to qualify their remarks.

More guarded these days than in their earlier, somewhat hysterical tracts, the Ehrlichs offer something for everyone in a rather bewildering number of scenarios which show concern for the poor as well as the rich, the Third World as well as the First, even Marxists as well as avowed conservatives. But almost every important passage in the book repeats the refrain that marks their earlier works: "Controlling population growth is critical."

The Ehrlichs' treatment of fundamental social issues, however, reveals the extent to which they come to terms with the status quo. Our democratic "market-based economies [are] so far the most successful political and economic systems human beings have ever devised." That there is a systemic relationship between "market-based" economy and the ruthless plundering of the planet hardly appears on the Ehrlichs' social horizon.

Naess is equally troubling in his solutions. As he weighs such alternative political philosophies as communism and anarchism, the father of deep ecology asserts, in his recently translated *Ecology, Community, and Lifestyle*, that deep ecology has an affinity with "contemporary nonviolent anarchism." But the reader stunned by this commitment to a libertarian alternative quickly learns that "with the enormous and exponentially increasing human population pressure and war or warlike conditions in many places, it seems inevitable to maintain some fairly strong central institutions"—or, put less obliquely than deep ecologists are wont to do, a "fairly strong" centralized state. Here, in fact, Naess's neo-Malthusianism and his pessimistic view of the human condition reinforce elitist beliefs in the ecology movement for state centralization and the use of coercion. The views of such deep ecologists as Christopher Manes, whose own colleagues regard him as an extremist, barely deserve serious discussion. Manes has welcomed the AIDS epidemic as a means of population control. Many mystical ecology writers echo his claim that "wilderness and not civilization is the real world."

One of the most strident condemnations of human beings as the source of the ecological crisis comes from James Lovelock, the architect of the "Gaia hypothesis," a mythopoeic notion that the Earth, personified as "Gaia" (the Greek goddess of our planet), is literally a living organism. In this theology, "we," needless to say, are not merely trivial and expendable but, as some Gaians have put it, parasitic "intelligent fleas" on the planet. For Lovelock, the word "we" replaces all distinctions between elites and their victims in a shared responsibility for present-day ecological ills.

"Our humanist concerns about the poor of the inner cities or the Third World," Lovelock declaims, "and our near-obscene obsession with death, suffering, and pain as if these were evils in themselves — these thoughts divert the mind from our gross and excessive domination of the natural world. Poverty and suffering are not sent; they are the consequences of what we do."

It is "when we drive our cars and listen to the radio bringing news of acid rain [that] we need to remind ourselves that we, personally, are the polluters." Accordingly, "we are therefore accountable, personally, for the destruction of the trees by photochemical smog and acid rain." The lowly consumer is seen as the real source of the ecological crisis, not the producers who orchestrate public tastes through the mass media and the corporations who own and ravage Lovelock's divine Gaia.

THE ECOLOGY MOVEMENT IS TOO IMPORTANT to allow itself to be taken over by airy mystics and reactionary misanthropes. The traditional labor movement, on which so many radicals placed their hopes for creating a new society, has withered, and in the United States the old-time populist movements have died with the agrarian strata that provided them with sizable followings. Rooseveltian liberalism's future hangs in the balance as a result of the Reagan-Bush assault on New Deal reforms. The cooptation of nearly every worthwhile cause, including conventional environmentalism itself, is symbolized by the ease with which corporations tout the slogan "Every Day is Earth Day!"

But the natural world itself is not cooptable. The complexity of organic and climatic processes still defies scientific control, just as the marketplace's drive to expand still defies social control. The conflict between the natural world and the present society has intensified over the past two decades. Ecological dislocations of massive proportions may well begin to overshadow the more sensational issues that make headlines today.

A decisive collision looms: On one side is the "grow-or-die" economy, lurching out of control. On the other, the fragile conditions necessary for the maintenance of advanced life-forms on this planet. This collision, in fact, confronts humanity itself with sharp alternatives: an ecological society structured around social ecology's ideal of a confederal, directly democratic, and ecologically oriented network of communities, or an authoritarian society in which humanity's interaction with the natural world will be structured around a command economics and politics. The third prospect, of course, is the immolation of humanity in a series of ecological and irreversible disasters.

For the ecology movement to become frivolous and allow itself to be guided by various sorts of mystics would be unpardonable — a tragedy of enormous proportions. Despite the dystopian atmosphere that seems to pervade much of the movement, its utopian vision of a democratic, rational, and ecological society is as viable today as it was a generation ago.

The misanthropic strain that runs through the movement in the name of biocentrism, antihumanism, Gaian consciousness, and neo-Malthusianism threatens to make ecology, in the broad sense of the term, the best candidate we have for a "dismal science." The attempt of many mystical ecologists to exculpate the present society for its role in famines, epidemics, poverty, and hunger serves the world's power elites as the most effective ideological defense for the extremes of wealth on the one side and poverty on the other.

It is not only the great mass of people who must make hard choices about humanity's future in a period of growing ecological dislocation; it is the ecology movement itself that must make hard choices about its sense of direction in a time of growing mystification.

The Population Myth

I

The "population problem" has a Phoenix-like existence: it rises from the ashes at least every generation and sometimes every decade or so. The prophecies are usually the same — namely, that human beings are populating the earth in "unprecedented numbers" and "devouring" its resources like a locust plague.

In the days of the Industrial Revolution, Thomas Malthus, an unsavory English parson, formulated his notorious "law of population" which asserts that while food supplies expand only arithmetically, population soars geometrically. Only by wars, famines, and disease (Malthus essentially argued) can a "balance" be struck: between population and food supplies. Malthus did not mean this to be an argument to foster human welfare; it was an unfeeling justification for the inhuman miseries inflicted on the mass of English people by land-grabbing aristocrats and exploitative "industrialists." True to the mean-spirited atmosphere of the times, Malthus opposed attempts to alleviate poverty because they would remove the limits imposed on "population growth" by prolonging the lives of the poor.

Malthus's "law" entered into Darwin's explanation of evolution and reemerged from biology as "social-Darwinism." Propounded vigorously in the U.S. and England a generation later, this theory reduced society to a "jungle," in effect, in which a "law of survival of the fittest" justified the wanton plundering of the world by the wealthy or the "fittest," while the laboring classes, dispossessed farmers, and Third World "savages" were reduced to penury, presumably because they were "unfit" to survive. The arrogance of bankers, industrialists, and colonialists in the "Gilded Age" at the turn of the century who dined on lavish dishes, while starved bodies were collected regularly in the city streets of the western world — all testified to a harsh class system that invoked "natural law" to justify the opulence enjoyed by the ruling few and the hunger suffered by the ruled many.

Barely a generation later, Malthusianism acquired an explicitly racist character. During the early twenties, when "Anglo-Saxon" racism peaked in the U.S. against "darker" peoples like Italians, Jews, and Eastern Europeans, the notion of "biological inferiority" led to explicitly exclusionary immigration laws that favored northern Europeans over other, presumably "subhuman" peoples. Malthusianism, now prefixed with a "neo" to render it more contemporary, thoroughly permeated this legislation. Population in the U.S. had to be "controlled" and American "cultural" (read: racial) purity had to be rescued — be it from the "Yellow Peril" of Asia or the "Dark Peril" of the Latin and Semitic worlds.

Nazism did not have to invent its racial imagery of sturdy "Aryans" beleaguered by "subhuman" dark people, particularly Jews. Hitler saw himself as the protector of a "northern European culture" from "Hebraic superstitions," to use the juicy language of a contemporary well-known Arizona writer — a "cultural" issue that was riddled by fascist sociobiology. From Hitler's "northern European" viewpoint, Europe was "overpopulated" in the 1930s and the continent's ethnic groups had to be sifted out according to their racial background. Hence the gas chambers and crematoriums of Auschwitz, the execution squads that followed the German army into Russia in the summer of 1941, and the systematic and mechanized slaughter of millions in a span of three or four years.

The Phoenix Rises Again

One would have thought that the Second World War and the ugly traditions that fed into it would create a deeper sense of humanity and a more sensitive regard for life — nonhuman as well as human. Judging from the way the "population problem" has surfaced again, however, we seem even more brutalized than ever. By the late 1940s, before the wartime dead had fully decayed, the neo-Malthusians were back at work — this time to object to the use of pesticides newly developed to eradicate malaria and antibiotics to control killing infections in the Third World. Even eminent biologists like William Vogt entered the fray, attacking modern medicine for preserving human life and predicting famines in Britain between 1948 and 1978 and imminent famine in Germany and Japan. The ugly debate was overshadowed by the Korean War and the blandly optimistic Eisenhower era, followed by the stormy sixties period with its message

31

of idealism, public service, and, if you please, "humanism." But the decade barely came to a close when neo-Malthusianism surfaced again — this time with grim books that warned of a "population bomb" and advocated an "ethics" of "triage" in which the nations that were recommended for U.S. aid seemed uncannily to fall on the American side of the "Cold War," irrespective of their population growth rates.

Viewed from a distance of two decades later, the predictions made by many neo-Malthusians seem almost insanely ridiculous. We were warned, often in the mass media, that by the 1980s, for example, artificial islands in the oceans would be needed to accommodate growing population densities on the continents. Our oil supplies, we were told with supreme certainty, would be completely depleted by the end of the century. Wars between starving peoples would ravage the planet, each nation seeking to plunder the hidden food stores of the others. By the late seventies, this "debate" took a welcome breather — but it has returned again like a phoenix dressed in the plumage of ecology. Given the hysteria and the exaggerated "predictions" of earlier such "debates," the tone today is a little calmer. But in some respects it is even more sinister. We have not been forced to turn our oceans into real estate, nor have we run out of oil, food, material resources — or neo-Malthusian prophets. But we are acquiring certain bad intellectual habits, and we are being rendered more gullible by a new kind of religiosity that goes under the name of "spirituality" with a new-style paganism and primitivism.

First of all, we are thinking more *quantitatively* than qualitatively now — all talk about "wholeness," "oneness," and "interconectedness" to the contrary notwithstanding. When we are told that the "population issue" is merely a "matter of numbers," as one Zero Population Growth writer put it, then the vast complexity of population growth and diminution is reduced to a mere numbers game, like the fluctuations of Dow Jones stock-market averages. Human beings, turned into digits, can thus be equated to fruitflies and their numbers narrowly correlated with food supply. This is "following the Dow" with a vengeance. Social research, as distinguished from the Voodoo ecology that passes under the name of "deep ecology" these days, reveals that human beings are highly *social* beings, not simply a species of mammals. Their behavior is profoundly conditioned by their social status, as people who belong to a particular gender, hierarchy, class group, ethnic tradition, community, or historical era, or adhere to any of a

32

variety of ideologies. They also have at their disposal powerful technologies, material resources, science, and a *naturally* endowed capacity for conceptual thought that provides them with a flexibility that few, if any, nonhuman beings possess, not to speak of mutable institutions and capacities for systematic group cooperation. Nothing, here, is more illusory than to aiming "follow the Dow." The bad intellectual habits of thinking out demographic — or even "resource" — issues in a linear, asocial, and ahistorical manner tends to enter into all ecological problems, thanks very much to the neo-Malthusians and to a "biocentrism" that equates people to nonhuman life-forms.

Secondly, by reducing us to studies of line graphs, bar graphs, and statistical tables, the neo-Malthusians literally freeze reality as it is. Their numerical extrapolations do not construct any reality that is new; they merely extend, statistic by statistic, what is basically old and given. They are "futurists" in the shallowest sense of the word, not "utopians" in the best sense. They teach us to accept society, behavior, and values as they *are*, not as they *should* be or even *could* be. This procedure places us under the tyranny of the status quo and divests us of any ability to think about radically changing the world. I have encountered very few books or articles written by neo-Malthusians that question whether we should live under money economy or a statist system of society, or be guided by profit-oriented behavior. There are books and articles aplenty that explain "how to" become a "morally responsible" banker, entrepreneur, landowner, "developer," or, for all I know, arms merchant. But whether the whole system called capitalism (forgive me!), be it corporate in the west or bureaucratic in the east, *must* be abandoned if we are to achieve an ecological society is rarely discussed. Thousands may rally around Earth First!'s idiotic slogan "Back to the Pleistocene!" but few conditioned by neo-Malthusian thinking will rally around the cry of the Left Greens — "Forward to an Ecological Society!"

Lastly, neo-Malthusian thinking is most backward in thinking out the *implications* of its demands. If we are concerned, today, and rightly so, about the sinister implications of registering AIDS victims, what are the totalitarian consequences of creating a Bureau of Population Control, as some Zero Population Growth wits suggested in the early 1970s? Imagine what consequences would follow from increasing the state's power over reproduction. Indeed, what areas of personal life would not be invaded by slowly enlarging the state's authority over our most intimate relations? Yet such demands in one form or another

33

have been raised by neo-Malthusians on grounds that lack the mental level needed to examine the Statistical Abstract of the United States.

The Social Roots of Hunger

This arithmetic mentality that disregards the social context of demographics is incredibly short-sighted. If we live in a "grow-or-die" capitalistic society in which accumulation is literally a law of economic survival and competition is the motor of "progress," anything we have to say about population causing the ecological crisis is basically meaningless. Under such a society the biosphere will eventually be destroyed whether five billion or fifty million people live on the planet. Competing firms in a "dog-eat-dog" market must out-produce each other if they are to remain in existence. They must plunder the soil, remove the earth's forests, kill off its wildlife, and pollute its air and waterways — not because their intentions are necessarily bad, although they usually are, hence the absurdity of the spiritualistic pablum in which Americans are currently immersed — but because they must simply survive. Only a radical restructuring of society as a whole, including its anti-ecological sensibilities, can remove this all-commanding social compulsion — not rituals, yoga, or encounter groups (valuable as some of these practices may be, no least in "improving" one's earning capacity and "power" to command).

But the most sinister feature of neo-Malthusianism is that it actively deflects us from dealing with the social origins of our ecological problems — indeed, places the blame for them on the victims of hunger rather than those who victimize them. If there is a "population problem" and famine in Africa, neo-Malthusianism blames the ordinary people for having too many children or insisting on living too long — much as Malthus nearly two centuries ago blamed England's poor. The viewpoint not only justifies privilege and degrades its victims; it brutalizes the neo-Malthusians as well.

And frankly — they often lie. Consider the issue of population and food supply in terms of mere numbers, and we step on a wild merry-go-round that does not support neo-Malthusian predictions of a decade ago, much less a generation ago. A typically neo-Malthusian stunt is to try to determine the "per capita consumption" of steel, oil, paper, chemicals, and the like of a nation by dividing the total tonnage consumed by the national population, such that every man, women, and child can be said to "consume" a resultant quantity gives us a picture that is blatantly false and functions as a sheer apologia for the upper classes. The steel that goes into constructing a battleship, the oil that is used to fuel a tank, and the paper that is used for ads hardly depicts the consumption of materials by ordinary people. Rather, the stuff is consumed by all the Pentagons of the world that help keep a "grow-or-die" economy in operation — goods, I may add, whose function is to destroy and whose destiny is to be destroyed. The shower of such "data" that descend upon us by neo-Malthusian writers is worse than obscurantist; it is vicious as the shopping malls that dump their toxic "consumer goods" on us and the costly highways that converge upon them. To ignore the fact that we are the victims of a vast, completely *entrapping* social order, which only a few can either control or escape from, is to literally deaden the political insight of ordinary people — whose "wants," of course, are blamed for every dislocation in our ecological dislocations.

On the demographic merry-do-round, the actual facts advanced by many neo-Malthusians are no less misleading. In the West, particularly in countries like Germany which neo-Malthusian prophets of the late 1940s warned would soar in population well beyond food supplies, birth rates have fallen beyond the national replacement rate. This is true of Denmark, Austria, Hungary, and indeed, much of Europe generally, including Catholic Italy and Ireland—where tradition, one would expect, would make for huge families. So traditions that foster large, predominantly male families, by which the high birth rates of India and China were explained, are not frozen in stone. The U.S., whose population the more hysterical neo-Malthusians of some two decades ago predicted would be obliged to live on oceanic rafts, is approaching zero population growth and, by now, it may be lower.*

---

*In fact, the most recent information is nothing less than startling: a report by the European Population Conference released in March 1993 predicts that Europe's overall population (in 20 countries) will drop from 449 million to 342 million by the middle of the next century. Catholic Spain and Italy will drop their fertility rate from about the 2.1 percent that they need to simply reproduce their population, to 1.2 percent. In Greece, the fertility rate has declined already from 2.2 percent to 1.4 percent in only a decade. On the whole, Europe's population is expected in the next fifty years to decline by a hundred million people, notwithstanding all the dire predictions on which Euro-Americans have been fed in the Malthusian literature of the past thirty years.

Nor is food supply lagging behind overall population growth. Cereal production rose by 12 percent since 1975, making it possible recently for even Bangladesh to drastically reduce its grain imports. The markets of western Asia are being flooded by Chinese corn. Even "barren" Saudi Arabia is selling off its accumulations of wheat, and in Finland, farmers are so overloaded with surplus wheat that they are turning it into mink fodder and glue. India, the so-called "worst case example," tripled its production of grain between 1950 and 1984. Its greatest problem at present is not population growth but the transportation of food from grain-surplus areas to grain-shortage ones — a major source of many Indian famines in the past.

Lester R. Brown of Worldwatch Institute divides the world "into countries where population growth is slow or nonexistent and where living conditions are improving, and those where population growth is rapid and living conditions are deteriorating or in imminent danger of doing so." One might easily conclude by the mere juxtaposition of Brown's phrases that declining living conditions are due solely to increasing population. Not so — if one looks closely at Brown's data as well as other sources. Much of the disparity between population growth and bad living conditions in Bangladesh, India, and Pakistan, for example, is due to patterns of land ownership. In southern Asia, some 30 million rural households own no land or very little, a figure that represents 40 percent of nearly all rural households in the subcontinent. Similar figures are emerging from Africa and Latin America. Land distribution is now so lopsided in the Third World in favor of commercial farming and a handful of elite landowners that one can no longer talk of a "population problem" without relating it to a class and social problem.

It would take several volumes to untangle the mixed threads that intertwine hunger with landownership, material improvements with declining population growth, technology with food production, the fragility of familial customs with the needs of women to achieve full personhood, internal civil wars (often financed by western imperialists) with famines — and the role of the World Bank and the International Monetary Fund with patterns of food cultivation. Westerners have only recently gained a small glimpse of the role of the IMF and World Bank in producing a terrible famine in the Sudan by obliging the country to shift from the cultivation of food in areas of rich soil to the cultivation of cotton.

This much must be emphasized: the "population issue" may well be the "litmus test" of one's ecological outlook, as the top honcho of Earth First!, David Foreman, has declared. Greens, ecologically oriented people, and radicals of all kinds will have to solve this problem with an acute sense of the social, not by playing a numbers game with human life and clouding up that social sense with thoroughly unreliable statistical extrapolations and apologias for corporate interests.

Nor can human beings be reduced to mere digits without reducing the world of life to digits — without replacing a decent regard for life, including human life, with a new eco-brutalism.

II

Before the 1970s, Malthusianism in its various historical forms claimed to rest on a statistically based formula: that population increases geometrically while food supply increases merely arithmetically. At the same time, anti-Malthusians could refute the formula by using factual data. Arguments between Malthusians and their opponents were thus based on empirical studies and rational explorations of the proliferation of human beings (despite the failure of Malthusians to introduce social factors that could either promote or inhibit population growth). Anti-Malthusians could empirically inventory the food that was available and take practical measures to increase the supply; food production could be assessed in terms of technological innovations that enhanced productivity. Land available for cultivation could be explored and put into production, often with minimal ecological damage. In short, pro- and anti-Malthusian arguments occurred within a rational arena of discourse and were subject to factual verification or refutation.

Today this situation seems to be changing radically. In an era of aggressive irrationalism and mysticism, empirical assessments are becoming increasingly irrelevant. The 1980s have seen the emergence of a *mystical* Malthusianism that does not draw on rationality to justify its own amorality and indifference to human suffering. The relationship between population and food is being thoroughly mystified. Herein lies a major problem in contemporary discussions on demographics.

Often, in fact, mystical Malthusianism surfaces as a pious concern about the human suffering that could be alleviated in presumably "overpopulated" areas through population control measures. This view can be as sincere as it is naive. But taken still further — as it commonly is — it can shade into a more sinister demographic ethos that argues for keeping those populations that are sinking into chronic famine from climbing into and overloading the human "lifeboat."

Biocentrism and Antihumanism

If earlier discussions on population were anchored in rational discourse, the current crop of Malthusians tend to mystify the relationship between population and the availability of food. Human beings are often seen as a "cancer" on the biosphere, a force for ecological dislocation and planetary destruction. The earth, in turn, is deified into an all-presiding "Gaia." "Gaia" is imparted with a mystical "will" and with divine powers that countervail abstract "humanity," bereft of any social divisions. "Gaia" can then visit upon this socially undifferentiated "us" retributive acts like famine, war, and, more currently in the Malthusian repertoire of vengeance, the AIDS epidemic. This view is not arguable; it is totally irrational.

Cast in this sinister form, the ecomystical neo-Malthusians of the post-sixties era tend to reduce human misfortune and its social sources to an ecotheistic apocalypse. The traditional Malthusian numbers game gives way to a modern morality drama in which the social sources of hunger are eclipsed by ineffable supernaturalistic ones. All this is done in the name of a theistic version of ecology — one that ironically is grounded in a crudely anthropomorphic personification of the earth as a divinity.

In principle, neo-Malthusians have long argued that people breed indefinitely, like lemmings, until they come up against "natural limits" imposed by the food supply. "Biocentrism" has provided a new wrinkle: the biocentric notion that human beings are "intrinsically" no different in "worth" from other animals lends a helping hand to Malthusianism. For after these "natural limits" are reached, "Gaia" dictates in some strange voice of "Her" own that starvation and death must ensue until population is reduced to the "carrying capacity" of a particular region.

By reducing social complexity to biological simplemindedness, biocentrism's broad identification of the "worth" of human beings and the "worth" of nonhumans denies to our species the enormous role that conceptual thought, values, culture, economic relationships, technology, and political institutions play in literally determining the "carrying capacity" of the planet on the one hand and in influencing human behavior in all its forms on the other. With startling mindless-

38

ness, socioeconomic factors are once again erased and their place is taken by a crude biologism that equates human "intrinsic worth" with that of lemmings, or — to use the animals of choice in the firmament of biocentrism — wolves, grizzly bears, cougars, and the like.

Two very important conclusions emerge from such one-dimensional thinking. The first stems from the equatability of human with nonhuman beings in terms of their "intrinsic worth." If human beings are no better "intrinsically" than lemmings, their premature death should be at least morally acceptable. Indeed, their death may even be biologically desirable in the "cosmic" scheme of things — that is, in order to keep "Gaia" on course and happy. Population control can then go beyond mere contraceptive advice to calculated neglect, fostering a "permissible" degree of famine and welcoming mass death from starvation. Such a situation occurred in Europe in the terrible Irish potato famine of the 1840s, when entire families perished due in no small part to Malthusian arguments against "intervention" in a "natural course of events."

Whether biocentrism's equation of the "intrinsic worth" of humans and lemmings will pave the ideological way to a future Auschwitz has yet to be seen. But the "moral" grounds for letting millions of people starve to death has been established with a vengeance, and it is arrogantly being advanced in the name of "ecology."

A second conclusion to which biocentrism lends itself is the deprecation of human intervention into nature as such. A blanket assumption exists among many biocentrists that human involvement in the natural world is generally bad and that "Gaia knows best." With this mystical assumption of a "knowing" Gaia that has a suprahuman personality of its own, the earthquake that killed tens of thousands of Armenians could easily be justified as "Gaia's response" to overpopulation.

Not surprisingly, assorted environmental groups that have made biocentrism a focal point in their philosophies tend toward a passive-receptive mysticism. Heidegger's numbing "openness to Being," Spinoza's fatalism, and various Asian theologies that enjoin us to yield to quietism have been used to becloud ecological issues with mystical overtones. We thus spin in an orbit of circular reasoning that subordinates human action to a supernatural world that is a product of human imagination. The result is that action as such becomes suspect irrespective of the social conditions in which it occurs.

Exactly at a time when we need the greatest clarity of thought and rational guidance to resolve the massive environmental dislocations that threaten the very stability of the planet, we are asked to bend before a completely mysterious "will" of "Gaia" that serves to paralyze human will and that darkens human perception with theistic chimeras. The ability to clearly think out the contradictions this mentality produces is blocked by theistic appeals to a mysticism that places a ban on logic and reason.

When a prominent ecological poet who has embraced deep ecology can claim (as he reportedly has) that for humanity to co-exist with grizzly bears and redwood trees, California's population will have to be reduced to one million people, another dilemma confronts us. It is no longer even an area's material "carrying capacity" that is to determine the human population it can sustain. "Carrying capacity" itself is literally dematerialized and redefined in an ecomystical way as "wilderness," which acquires suprahuman, even mysterious qualities of its own. No longer are people to crowd wilderness; rather wilderness is expected to crowd out people.

This counterposition of "primal" wilderness to humanity and to humanity's social "second nature" is completely atavistic. The view pivots on a myth that humanity is a stranger to natural evolution — indeed, that humanity's social "second nature" has no relationship to biology's presumably enchanted "first nature." To the Enlightenment of two centuries ago, humanity — at least, potentially — was the very voice of nature, and its place in nature utterly noble insofar as society was rational and humane.

The Mystical Malthusians

Today we are beginning to hear a new message. "The human race could go extinct," declares Dave Foreman, "and I, for one, would not shed any tears." Absurd as it may be, this message is not a rarity. Indeed, it is implicit in much of the thought that exists among the ecomystics and ecotheists.

What is important is that when grizzly bears can be placed on a par with human beings in the name of biocentrism — and I am surely not trying to make a case for the "extermination" of bears — we are witnessing not a greater sensitivity to life in general but a desensitization of the mind to human agony, consciousness, and personality, and to the potentiality of human beings to know and to understand that no other life-form can approximate. In an era of sweeping depersonalization and irrationalism, the value of human personality and human rationality counts less and less.

40

Reverence for nature, even respect for nonhuman life, provides no guarantee that humans will be included in the "life-oriented" mythos, the present crop of ecomystics and ecotheists to the contrary notwithstanding. The classical example of this is what Robert A. Pois has called an "ingenuous permutation of mysticism" in the Nazi movement. (Nazism, alas, was more than ingenuous., Hitler's *Mein Kampf* registered the stern, indeed "cosmic" view "that this planet once moved through the ether for millions of years without human beings, and it can do so again someday if men forget that they owe their higher existence, not to the ideas of a few crazy ideologists, but to the knowledge and ruthless application of Nature's stern and rigid laws." Alfred Rosenberg, the ideologist par excellence of Nazism, railed against Jewish "dualism" and avowed a neopagan pantheism "for a bridging of the gap between spirit and matter through deification of nature," to cite Pois's summary. This kind of language can be found at varying levels of intensity in the writings of deep ecologists, ecomystics, and ecotheists today, who would certainly eschew any association with Nazism and who would avow their innocence in fostering the cultural legacy they are creating.

Heinrich Himmler, who deployed the entire machinery of the SS in a vast operation to systematically kill millions of people, held this view with a vengeance. "Man," he told his SS leaders in Berlin in June 1942, at the height of the Nazis' extermination operations, "is nothing special." Ironically, his icy rejection of humanism found its fervent counterpart in his passionate love of animal life. Thus Himmler complained to a hunter, one Felix Kersten, "How can you find pleasure, Herr Kersten, in shooting from behind cover at poor creatures browsing on the edge of a wood, innocent, defenseless, and unsuspecting? It's really pure murder. Nature is so marvelously beautiful and every animal has a right to live." Such a passion for animal "rights" is often the opposite side of the misanthropic coin. Indeed, hatred of humanity has often reinforced adulation of animals, just as hatred of civilization has often reinforced a hypersentimental "naturalism."

This shadowy side of suprahuman "naturalism" suggests the perilous ground on which many ecomystics, ecotheists, and deep ecologists are walking and the dangers of de-sensitizing an already "minimalized" public, to use Christopher Lasch's term. As the late Edward Abbey's denunciations of Latin "genetic inferiority" and even "Hebraic superstitions" suggest, the mystical Malthusians themselves are not immune to the dangerous brew. The brew becomes highly explosive when it is mixed with a mysticism that supplants humanity's potentiality to be a rational voice of nature with an all-presiding "Gaia," an ecotheism that denies human beings their unique place in nature.

Reverence for *nature* is no guarantee of reverence for the world of life *generally*, and reverence for nonhuman life is no guarantee that human life will receive the respect it deserves. This is especially true when reverence is rooted in deification—and when a supine reverence becomes a substitute for social critique and social action.

Demography and Society

It was Marx who made the firm observation that every society has its own "law of population." When the bourgeoisie needed labor in its early years to operate its industrial innovations, human life became increasingly "sacred" and the death penalty was increasingly reserved for homicidal acts. Before then, however, a woman in Boston had actually been hanged merely for stealing a pair of shoes. Today, in an era of automatic and automated devices, human life again tends to become cheap — all pieties about the horrors of war to the contrary notwithstanding. A social logic that involved depopulation, mingled with a pathological anti-Semitism, guided Hitler even more than his mystical "naturalism." Demographic policy is always an expression of social policy and the type of society in which a given population lives.

The most disquieting feature of deep ecology theorists, Earth First! leaders, ecomystics, and ecotheists is the extent to which they nullify the importance of social factors in dealing with ecological and demographic issues — even as they embody them in some of their most mystified middle-class forms. This is convenient, both in terms of the ease with which their views are accepted in a period of social reaction and in the stark simplicity of their views in a period of naivete and social illiteracy.

William Petersen, a responsible demographer, has carefully nuanced what he calls "Some Home Truths About Population" in a recent issue of the *American Scholar*. Political factors, he points out, may play a larger role in recent famines than economic or even environmental ones. "Mozambique, recently named the poorest country in the world, has a fertile soil, valuable ores, and a fine coastline," Petersen observes. "That its GNP has fallen by half over the past five years and its foreign debt has risen by $2.3 billion, one must ascribe to its Communist government and the destabilizing efforts of neighboring South Africa. Of the population of roughly fourteen million, more than one person in ten is a would-be refugee, on the road fleeing civil war but finding no refuge anywhere."

Even more striking is the case of the Sudan, a land once celebrated for its agricultural fecundity. The Sudan is currently an appalling example of mismanagement, largely as a result of a British colonialist legacy of commitment to the cultivation of cotton and to World Bank loans for the development of agribusiness. Pressure by the Bank for increased cotton production in the late 1970s to offset balance-of-payment problems, the impact of rising oil prices on highly mechanized agricultural practices, and a considerable decline in home-grown food reserves — all combined to produce one of the most ghastly famines in northern Africa. The interaction of declining world prices for cotton, interference by the World Bank, and attempts to promote the sale of American wheat — a cereal that could have been grown in the Sudan if the country had not been forced to cultivate crops for the world market — claimed countless lives from hunger and produced massive social demoralization at home.

This drama, usually explained by the Malthusians as "evidence" of the dangers of population growth or by ecomystics as an apocalyptic visitation by "Gaia" for presumably sinful acts of abuse to the earth, is played out throughout much of the Third World. Class conflicts, which may very well lie at the root of the problems that face hungry people, are transmuted by the Malthusians into demographic ones in which starving country folk are pitted against impoverished townspeople, and landless refugees against nearly landless cultiva-tors of small plots — all of which immunizes the World Bank, American agribusiness, and a compradore bourgeoisie to criticism.

Even in the First World, where demographic profiles reveal a growing proportion of older people over younger ones, lobbies like Americans for Generational Equity (AGE) threaten to open a divide between recipients of social security and the young adults who presumably "pay the bill." Almost nothing is said about the economic system, the corporations, or the madcap expenditures for armaments and research into "life control" that devour vast revenues and invalu-able resources.

Population may soar for reasons that have less to do with repro-ductive biology than with capitalist economics. Destroy a traditional culture — its values, beliefs, and sense of identity — and population increases may even outpace its high preindustrial death rates. Life expectancy may even decline while absolute numbers of people rise significantly. This occurred during the worst years of the Industrial Revolution amidst major tuberculosis and cholera pandemics, not to speak of monstrous working conditions that repeatedly thinned out the ranks of the newly emerging proletariat. Ecology, the "carrying capacity" of a region, and least of all "Gaia" have very little to do with social demoralization and the breakdown of cultural restraints on reproduction. Economics and the exploitation of displaced agrarian folk are the really decisive factors, mundane as they may seem in the "cosmic" world of ecomysticism and deep ecology.

But conditions can stabilize and, given a higher quality of life, yield a relatively stable demographic situation. In more recent times, entirely new factors have emerged that may give rise to negative population growth. I refer not only to a desire for small families and more cultivated lifestyles, and concern for the development of the individual child rather than a large number of siblings, but, above all, women's liberation movements and the aspirations of young women to be more than reproductive factories.

In demographic transition, changes from traditional agrarian economies to modern industrial and urbanized ones involve a change from conditions of high fertility and morality to those of low fertility and mortality. Demographic transition has been called by George J. Stolnitz, a cautious demographer, "the most sweeping and best-documented historical trend of modern times." What should be added to this conclusion is the need to improve the living conditions of people who make this transition — generally, an improvement brought about by the labor movement and socially concerned educators, sanitarians, health workers, and radical organizations. If demographic transition has not occurred in the Third World (as a population-bomber like David Brower has suggested), it is largely because semifeudal elites, military satraps, and a pernicious domestic bourgeoisie have harshly repressed movements for social change. It is evidence of the incredible myopia and intellectual crudity of deep ecology, ecomystics, and ecotheistic acolytes that the notion of demographic transition has recently been written off as inoperative, with no attempt to account for the festering shantytowns that surround some of the largest Third World cities.

Will Ecology Become a Cruel Discipline?

Divested of its social core, ecology can easily become a cruel discipline. Neo-Malthusians — contemporary no less than earlier ones — often exhibited a meanness of spirit that completely fits into the "me-too" Yuppie atmosphere of the eighties. Consider the following passages from William Vogt's *The Road to Survival*, the work of an eminent biologist that was published a generation ago. Anticipating more recent prescriptions, he avowed, "Large scale bacterial warfare would be an effective, if drastic, means of bringing back the earth's forests and grasslands." And in a more thumping passage well on into the book, he adds that the Food and Agriculture Organization of the United Nations "should not ship food to keep alive ten million Indians and Chinese this year, so that fifty million may die five years hence" — a gothic "generosity" that recurs throughout the Malthusian literature of the eighties.

These recipes essentially faded away as social unrest in the Third World itself surged up and rendered them untenable in the Cold War's demands for new political alignments abroad. The year 1968, however, was not only a climactic one in radical politics but an initiating one in reactionary politics. In that year, perhaps one of the earliest manifestations of the move to the right was the publication and staggering popularity of Paul R. Ehrlich's *The Population Bomb*, which ran through thirteen printings in only two years and gave birth to an army of population bombers.

For deep ecologists like George Sessions and Bill Devall to praise Ehrlich as a "radical ecologist" verges on black humor. The book still reads like a hurricane on the loose, a maddening blowout of spleen and venom. From a sketch of human misery in Delhi in which "people" (the word is used sneeringly to open almost every sentence on the first page) are seen as "visiting, arguing, and screaming," as "thrusting their hands through the taxi windows, begging . . . defecating and urinating," Ehrlich and family seem to swoon with disgust over "people, people, people, people, people." We have a sense — one by no means felt by most of the book's American readers — that we have entered another world from Ehrlich's sublime campus at Stanford University. Thus it was, Ehrlich tells us, that he came to know "the *feel* of overpopulation," in sum, attained the sense of disgust that pervades the entire work.

Thereafter, our "radical ecologist" runs riot with his misanthropy. The Third World is depersonalized into computer-age abbreviations like "UDCs" (underdeveloped countries); medical advances are described as forms of "death control"; and pollution problems "all can be traced to *too many people*" (Ehrlich's emphasis). Terrifying scenarios engage in a ballet with each other that is strangely lacking in noticeable references to capitalism or to the impact of an ever-expanding grow-or-die market economy. Apart from the usual demand for increased tax burdens on those who "breed" excessively, contraception, and educational work on family planning, a centerpiece of the book is Ehrlich's demand for a "powerful governmental agency." Accordingly: "A federal Department of Population and Environment (DPE) should be set up with the power to take *whatever steps are necessary* to establish a reasonable population size in the United States and to put an end to the steady deterioration of our environment." (The book enjoyed a great vogue, incidentally, during the Nixon administration.) Lest we waver in our resolve, Ehrlich reminds us: "The *policemen* against environmental deterioration must be the *powerful* Department of Population and Environment mentioned above" (my emphasis in both quotations). Happily for the "business community," Ehrlich quotes one J. J. Spengler to the effect that "It is high time, therefore, that business cease looking upon the stork as a bird of good omen."

The Population Bomb climaxes in a favorable description of what is now known as "the ethics of triage." Drawn from warfare, "the idea briefly is this: When casualties crowd a dressing station to the point where all cannot be cared for by the limited medical staff, some decisions must be made on who will be treated. For this purpose the triage system of classification was developed. All incoming casualites are placed in one of three classes. In the first class are those who will die regardless of treatment. In the second are those who will survive regardless of treatment. The third contains those who can be saved only if they are given prompt treatment." The presumption, here, is that the medical staff is "limited" and the diagnosis of a person is free of political considerations like the country's alignment in the Cold War.

Among neo-Malthusians, hardly any attempt is made to think out premises, indeed, to ask what *follows* from a given statement. If all life forms have the same "intrinsic worth" as deep ecologists contend, can we impart to malarial mosquitoes or tsetse flies the same "right" to exist that we accord to whales and grizzly bears? Can a bacterium that could threaten to exterminate chimpanzees be left to do so because it too has "intrinsic worth" and, perhaps, because human beings who can control a lethal disease of chimps should not "interfere" with the

46

mystical workings of "Gaia"? *Who* is to decide what constitutes "valid" interference by human beings in nature and what is invalid? To *what* extent can conscious, rational, and moral human intervention in nature be seriously regarded as "unnatural," especially if one considers the vast evolution of life toward greater subjectivity and ultimately human intellectuality? To *what* extent can humanity itself be viewed simply as a single species, when social life is riddled by hierarchy and domination, gender biases, class exploitation, and ethnic discrimination?

Demography and Society

The importance of viewing demography in social terms is all the more apparent when we ask: would the grow-or-die economy of capitalism cease to plunder the planet if the world's population were reduced to a tenth of its present numbers? Would lumber companies, mining concerns, oil cartels, and agribusiness render redwood and Douglas fir forests safer for grizzly bears if — given capitalism's need to accumulate and produce for their own sake — California's population were reduced to one million people?

The answer to these questions is a categorical no. Vast bison herds were exterminated on the western plains long before the plains were settled by farmers or used extensively by ranchers — indeed, when the American population barely exceeded some sixty million people. These great herds were not crowded out by human settlements, let alone by excessive population. We have yet to determine what constitutes the "carrying capacity" of the planet for even larger human populations, just as we lack any certainty, given the present predatory economy, about what constitutes a strictly numerical balance between reduced human numbers and a given ecological area. All the statistics that are projected by demographers, today, are heavily conditioned by various values that remain unexplored, such as the desire of some people for pristine "wilderness," or even mere open land, a pastoral concept of nature, and a love of cultivated land. Indeed, human taste has varied so widely over the centuries with respect to what constitutes "nature" that we may well ask whether it is ever "natural" to exclude the human species — a distinct product of natural evolution — from our conceptions of the natural world, including from so-called "pristine" wilderness areas.

This much seems reasonably clear: a "wilderness" that has to be protected from human intervention is already a product of human intervention. It is no more "wild" if it has to be guarded than an aboriginal culture is truly authentic if it has to be shielded from the impacts of "civilization." We have long since left the remote world when purely biological factors determined evolution and the destiny of most species on the planet. Until these problematic areas that influence modern thinking on demographics are clarified and their social implications—indeed, underpinnings—are fully explored, the neo-Malthusians are operating in a theoretical vacuum and filling it with extremely perilous ideas. Indeed it is a short step from writing anti-Semitic letters to Jewish furriers in the name of "animal rights" to scrawling swastikas on Jewish temples and synagogues.

Ecomystics, ecotheists, and deep ecologists create a very troubling situation when they introduce completely arbitrary factors into discussions on demographics. "Gaia" becomes whatever one chooses to make of "Her": demonic avenger or a loving mother; a homeostatic mechanism or a mystical spirit; a personified deity or a pantheistic principle. In all of these roles, "She" can easily be used to advance a misanthropic message of human self-hatred or worse, a hatred of specific ethnic groups and cultures — with consequences that cannot be foreseen even by "Her" most loving, well-meaning, and pacific acolytes. It is this utterly *arbitrary* feature of ecomystical and ecotheistic thinking, often divested of all social content, that makes most "new paradigm" discussions of the population issue not only very troubling but potentially very sinister.

Green Perspectives is a social ecology bulletin published by the Social Ecology Project on a monthly basis whenever possible. For a subscription to ten issues, please send $10.00 to P.O. Box 111, Burlington, VT 05402. "The Population Myth" first appeared in *Green Perspectives* in 1988-89.

SOCIOBIOLOGY OR SOCIAL ECOLOGY

I

The interface between nature and society has been a haunting philosophical, ethical, and cultural problem for thousands of years. Indeed, that it constitutes the stuff from which naive myths and thoughtful moral credos have been formed for ages is a fact we are seldom permitted to forget, if only in a fashion that is patronizing to presumably less "sophisticated" cultures. After all, were not the earliest religions "mere" nature religions and the earliest philosophies "mere" nature philosophies? As far back as we can search into humanity's rich reservoir of intuitions and rational formulas, our relationship to nature — indeed, humanity's place in nature — has been a central theme of ideas and sensibility. To seek an objective grounding for reason and ethics that is more than crudely instrumental and subjectively relativistic has been the alluring goal of human thought for an incalculable period of time.

It was only with the opening of the Christian era and, centuries later, with the birth of its wayward child, the Renaissance, that this haunting interface was slowly edged out of the realm of human speculation. Christianity's intensely anti-naturalistic bias essentially replaced an earlier, richly formed idea of nature with a colorless Supernature as ruthlessly as the late Renaissance philosophers and scientists (notably, Descartes and Galileo) were to replace organic strategies of knowledge with harshly mechanistic ones — an umbilical cord between the cathedral and the laboratory that Bacon was to sanctify in his utopian House of Saloman. The results of these ideological changes were more fateful than their creators realized. Human thought was completely deflected from a rational inquiry into the relationship of society to nature — one free of the religious and philosophical archaisms of the past — into a narrowly instrumental, means-end rationalism. A distinctly philosophical credo was established in the name of the new science that was no less metaphysical in its presuppositions than the archaic metaphysics of classical thought: a vision of nature as "mute," "blind," and intelligible only in mathematical terms; a vision of natural history as strictly fortuitous; and perhaps most decisively, an ethical strategy that was grounded not in objectivity and a search for the inherent self-organizing attributes that impart meaning to nature and society but in "effectiveness" and in a logical calculus of efficiency that could be justified only in terms of "success" and personal proclivities. Ironically, the Renaissance vision of society's interface with nature had not removed morality as such from the issue; it had replaced a *committed* vision of right and wrong with an essentially *uncommitted* one. In its *scientistic* "value-free" but instrumental approach to society, it had in fact provided a means-end rationalism that could as easily justify fascism as it could socialism — and, sadly enough, a uniquely vulgar interpretation of "anarchism" that tends to erupt from time to time like a fetid ulcer in the Anglo-American culture region.* Granted that medieval teleology with its rigid mythos of an inexorable "final cause" had permeated speculative thought with the autocracy of a preordained religious destiny; Renaissance mechanism, in turn, lifted the burden of "final cause" only to replace it with an equally rigid mythos of "efficient cause" with its unyielding determinism and its autocracy of reductionism. In neither case was freedom served and domination banished. Rather, the same commitment to a metaphysics of unswerving determinism was reinforced over more organic concepts of the world that gave it meaning without the all-presiding presence of a deity or a machine.

These general remarks are not made idly. They are indispensable for understanding two conflicting interpretations of the interface between nature and society: sociobiology and social ecology. The historic crisis in reason, science, and ethics which has reached such acuity in recent years — with Renaissance mechanism's underlying tenets of instrumental rationalism, of quantification as the "language" of science, and of physics as its "paradigm" — feeds into a more

---

* Consider, for example, an article in defense of contemporary sociobiology in a recent issue of *The North American Anarchist* (renamed *Strike*) which deals with nature as "blind . . . meaningless . . . mute" and the like, and rehabilitates all the vulgarities of mechanical materialism à la Mettrie or Moleschott. I quote from memory but with a deep concern that this kind of intellectual primitivism may find its place as "materialistic" or "anti-theological" in anarchist ideas. We have as much to fear from a kneejerk form of scientism and behaviorism, not to speak of sociobiology, as we have from theology and mysticism.

compelling material crisis: the unprecedented ecological deterioration that threatens the very integrity of complex life-forms, including humanity, None of the critics of instrumentalism, quantification, and reductionism, from the phenomenologists to the critical theorists of the Frankfurt School, could have anticipated that nature itself would raise problems that once seemed confined to the ideological and social realms. The massive disequilibrium between humanity and nature created by a terrifying, exploitative society has thus created the need for a new agenda with roots in an admittedly very old tradition. We are once again faced with the problem of how society emerged from nature, the continuities and discontinuities that exist between the two, the development of a sensibility and of social relations that accord with these distinctions (including reason and science as well as alternative communities and technics), and finally, an ethics that is grounded as much in nature as it is in human rationality. In short, the old ghosts, seemingly dispelled by the Cartesian and Galilean tradition, have come back to haunt us — not, let me emphasize, for want of the obscurantist ideological needs that many archaic religions and philosophical systems were meant to satisfy, but for want of a *new perspective* on humanity and nature that can resolve the ecological crisis of our times.

It is against this much larger background of ideas and problems that sociobiology's sudden emergence and utterly reactionary content should be evaluated. The idea that society has roots in nature is not new. Until the nineteenth century, the term "natural philosophy" was used as a synonym for the term "science." Hegel's recovery of Aristotelian physics and biology from the theological trappings of the medieval Schoolmen (all his own prejudices and idealistic nonsense aside) exercised an enormous influence in the academic world as a *qualitative basis* for the quantitative sciences. Nor can we ignore the influence "dialectical materialism" has exercised even if only as a source of sharp intellectual contention. Issues like "teleology" and "purposiveness" in nature, however simplistically defined, are central concerns of modern systems theory and neo-positivistic philosophies of science, not simply of Teilhard de Chardin's quasi-theological ruminations on orthogenesis.

Sociobiology has oozed into these major intellectual crevices of our times like some ideological pus from a suppurating ulcer. It is evidence not of a cure to the problems that have emerged but of the disease itself. It would be a serious error to view sociobiology merely as part of a persisting endeavor to relate attributes of the organic world to the social or to explore the biological roots of society in terms of their continuities and discontinuities. This project is thousands of years old and has had a highly diversified life of its own. It extends back to the pre-Socratics and has acquired its most conventional form in a neo-Bergsonian vitalism and in systems theory. Sociobiology, as the term is currently used, is a very specific creature in its own right. More precisely, it is not a discipline; it is a movement, no less offensive in its crudities than social-Darwinism. Considered as a movement, sociobiology's manifesto can largely be regarded as E. O. Wilson's *Sociobiology: The New Synthesis*. Its specificity as a "New Synthesis" cannot be ignored. The work of Wilson and his collaborators, some of whose views approximate pure fascism, must be singled out as a *new* attempt to deal with the interface between biology and society, indeed, to give it the halo of a scientific authority that defies mere theorizing and speculation. We are no longer dealing, here, with the Ionian philosophers, Parmenides' and Heraklitos' "Dike," Plato's *Demiurgos*, Aristotle's tour de force in the *Physics* and the *scala natura*, Demokritos, Epikurus, the Stoics, or, for that matter, with Bruno, Kepler, Leibnitz, Hegel, Kropotkin, Bergson, and the like. We are talking of a love affair between a new, presumably very "modern" and "sophisticated" group of largely Anglo-American biologists and ethologists on the one hand and genes on the other. The opening chapter of Wilson's *Sociobiology* is titled "The Morality of the Gene" — and it is the book's reductionist and ugly ethos, viewed as a key to society and human behavior, that must never be permitted to elude us.

Accolades for Wilson's "civility" and "appropriate sense of humor" (to use Ashley Montagu's flattering characterization) in the face of very heated attacks upon his views do not justify an equal degree of civility and humor from his critics. There is nothing very civil about sociobiology and certainly nothing very funny about its conclusions. Indeed, the critical response to *Sociobiology* has been largely favorable. This cordial, often enthusiastic reception has been extended not only by members of the scientific community but by a wide range of the entire political spectrum from writers for Britain's fascist National Front to their counterparts in the happily defunct "Anarcho-Communist Federation of North America."

Wilson, however, does not need reborn fascists and self-styled anarchists to speak on his behalf. He is more articulate and coherent than many of his fervent supporters. The vividness of his emphasis on aggression, hierarchy, domination, territoriality, and competition as genetically innate to all life-forms is so defiantly brash that it has become conventional to critically single out these issues. In Wilson's writings, very few of the less savory aspects of animal and human behavior are free of a genetic pedigree, and with this pedigree they become biologically inevitable, in fact, adaptative to survival. Such awkward traits as altruism and such patently cultural attributes as sympathy emerge as problems, not socially motivated achievements, that the sociobiologist must absorb into the "morality of the gene." Enough has been written on Wilson's image of animal and human behavior to focus, here, on the more substantive issues raised by his and his colleagues' works.

Nevertheless, it is difficult to ignore Wilson's intellectual strategy. *Sociobiology* is shrewdly riddled by a sufficient number of second thoughts and qualifications to obscure the viciousness of its thesis. More cautious than such rabidly reactionary acolytes as Richard Dawkins, whose *Selfish Gene* has been characterized by so prudent a critic as Mary Midgley as the "work of an uncritical philosophic egoist," Wilson is careful to take note of the "limits of aggression," to poetize over the "field of righteousness," and to acknowledge the "plasticity of [human] social organization," with due deference to "sharing" and "bonding." But wherever Wilson seems to relax his genetic determinism in the realm of culture, he rarely displaces it completely. *Sociobiology* unceasingly stakes out limits to non-genetic autonomy. Biological determinism, specifically in its crassest genic form, is not merely a massive emphasis but an all-encompassing gospel. Whatever seems to challenge this calling is conveniently removed from the purview of the book. It becomes non-existent or didactically dismissed when it cannot be cajoled by all means — fair or foul — into a genic "paradigm."

And Wilson is by no means so prudent as to abandon foul means. We shall have occasion to see that his genetics, far from being on the cutting edge of genic theories, is in fact rather archaic and shopworn. Nor is his ethological data free of rather cynical distortion. James C. King, in his highly informative and restrained criticism of sociobiology, notes that wedded to Wilson's "single-gene analysis and genetic determinism is . . . an emphasis on conflict and violence." Wilson's nature, including much of human nature, is ravaged by claw and fang, indeed, by a pervasive social-Darwinism that is denied rhetorically only to be smuggled in substantively. This high-pitch of conflict and violence is far from supported by the scientific "objectivity" that is supposed to render the sociobiological synthesis so new.

A few examples are worth citing. Wilson's use of Schneirla's data on cats to demonstrate that parent-offspring relations are marked by conflict in weaning kittens from their mother has been justly characterized by King as "close to distortion and points up the predisposition of the sociobiologist to see conflict everywhere." As it turns out, Schneirla's account of this relationship is highly complex: it involves an intricate alternation of lessening concern between the feline parent and its offspring which ultimately yields a condition of interdependence rather than hostility. Even more disconcerting is Wilson's misuse of G.B. Schaller's data on the Serengeti lions. Adducing Schaller's work as evidence, Wilson brashly contends that lion "cubs are sometimes killed and eaten during territorial disputes" — and there the account of high cub mortality is permitted to rest. Actually Schaller and other authoritative ethologists attribute this high mortality rate mainly to parental neglect rather than cannibalism. Acolytes of sociobiology are all the more revealing of their biases when the data around a particular issue is disputable. Almost invariably their interpretations of ambiguous facts fall on the side of aggression, violence, infanticide, and conflict. The more gory the trait, the more likely it is to invite the purple prose of dogma rather than the staid language of "scientific objectivity."

All of this raises what is most crucial in sociobiology's image of nature — of life as it is formed, of life-forms interacting with each other and their abiotic environment, and ultimately of human nature as it is formed biologically and culturally. Wilson's image of nature, like Freud's, is unequivocally Hobbesian, a *bellum omnium contra omnes*. Methodologically, Wilson is reductionist. What is no less significant, he has an epistemology that renders his subject matter inherently unruly and impervious to explanations that elicit any traits of an immanently symbiotic and mutualistic nature. Human nature, however one chooses to describe it, is an effect rather than a cause. It is largely the result of the ever-domineering gene. That there are immanent, self-organizing, and — yes, let us use the dreaded word, *harmonizing* — as well as conflicted— tendencies in nature and society which could form the bases of a new biosocial approach to evolution remain notions that are essentially alien to Wilson's sociobiology.

It would be very useful, if space permitted, to explore Wilson's definitions of "society," "hierarchy," "dominance," "aggregation," "band," "caste," "communal," "competition," and like words that clearly reveal his orientation toward biosocial, evolutionary, socially structured, and ethical phenomena. What is striking about most of these definitions is that, where they have social implications, Wilson firmly contains them by unrelenting, often rigid, *biological* terms. On the other hand, where their biological implications almost beg for interpretation, they are equated with biologically biased *social* terms. What I am saying is that Wilson's ruthless reduction of social phenomena to biology in general and genetics in particular is obscurantist by definition in the literal sense — by his definition of key terms that enter into his book. He renders it difficult for anyone but the most sophisticated reader to use language in such a way that it can reveal the discontinuities as well as the continuities between biology and society. Even more irritating, Wilson so crassly biases his language that the dialectical relations between these continuities and discontinuities become elusive. The perceptive reader, in effect, is stranded on a sociobiological island where it is virtually impossible to consume anything but sand and salt.

This becomes evident when one turns to Wilson's definition of "society." A "society" in *Sociobiology* is a "group of individuals belonging to the same species and organized in a cooperative manner." The diagnostic criterion is reciprocal communication of a cooperative nature, extending beyond mere sexual activities — after which mouthful of words, Wilson dispatches the reader to Chapter Two of the book.

It is vitally necessary, unless one is a mindless acolyte, to know what Wilson means "organized" and "cooperative" here — two culturally, philosophically, and ethically laden terms that have far-reaching implications in social theory, not to speak of biology, where their meanings may differ drastically in the same species (such as baboons) in different ecosystems. One finds, in fact, that Chapter Two in no way clarifies the meaning of these highly charged terms. If anything, Wilson wanders all over the place. We no more know what "cooperation" means than we know the meaning of "organization." Wilson's definitions are as arbitrary as they are intuitive. We are urged, in fact, to define the terms "society" and "social" sufficiently "broadly in order to prevent the exclusion of many interesting (!) phenomena" — in whose opinion and by what criteria Wilson fails to explain.

Accordingly, Wilson is now free to opine on any phenomenon that captures his fancy — a totally legitimate right if sociobiology is a purely speculative theory but certainly intellectually outrageous if it is (as its acolytes demand) a "science." We are told, for example, that "swarms of courting males" are not "true societies" because they are "often drawn together by mutually attractive stimuli, but if they interact in no other way it seems excessive to refer to them by a term stronger than aggregation." By contrast, Wilson declares, bird flocks, wolf packs, and locust swarms are "good examples of true elementary societies." So are parent-offspring relationships if they "communicate reciprocally" because they have "often complex and serve multiple functions." Indeed "in many groups of organisms, from the social insects to the primates, the most advanced societies appear to have evolved from family units."

We must pause, here, to examine this fascinating muddle of ideas and categories. If society is to be so broadly defined that it includes bird flocks and locust swarms but not swarms of courting males, by what solid criteria other than Wilson's cavalier use of the word "excessive" are the former distinguished from the latter? All three flocks and swarms are united by some kind of "attractive stimuli"; they perform some kind of "function" and in the "broadest sense" are apparently "cooperating" to fulfill that "function." Taken at face value, Wilson has assigned the notion of internal organization — that is, some vague idea of "group behavior" — as his criterion for distinguishing a "society" from a mere "aggregation." But the swarming of courting males, or for that matter, the winter congregation of rattlesnakes and ladybird beetles (which Wilson also consigns to the status of "aggregations") are forms of "group behavior" in themselves. The fact is that Wilson's criteria in distinguishing "society" from "aggregation" are matters of degree rather than of kind. Courting males, wintering rattlesnakes and ladybird beetles are not *sufficiently* "organized" and do not *sufficiently* "cooperate" for Wilson's tastes to qualify in his sovereign opinion as "true societies"; hence by no standards other than his personal judgment are they reduced to "aggregations."

I have emphasized Wilson's biases primarily to argue several key points. Minimally, with bias as its criterion, sociobiology holds no promise of becoming even a reasonably precise science. In fact, it rates very badly as a "new synthesis." Indeed, its claim becomes all the more arrogant because it professes to have achieved an "objectivity" that is ostensibly lacking in the "metaphysical" orientations it explicitly opposes. Actually, one encounters arbitrary judgments everywhere throughout the sociobiological literature and the writings of Wilson's ethological allies. But what is more important — and often less apparent — is that Wilson is seeking something that he never fully finds in the animal world: society conceived as an *institutionalized* system of relationships — that is to say, the conscious fabrication of associative behavior. Animals may form loosely or tightly aggregated *communities*, but differences in *degree* of aggregation do not determine whether they are *societies*. They merely determine how stable these aggregations are as communities and the range of functions they perform.

The need to distinguish society, a uniquely *human* attribute, from community, a generally organic attribute (which, as we shall see, can even apply to the organization of a single cell), is by no means academic. Indeed, the tendency to confuse the two — an error that is easily made because every society is necessarily also a community — mars the work of such widely disparate thinkers as Marx, Darwin, Kropotkin, and, of course, Wilson. We can ill afford this confusion without yielding the most disconcerting results. A community organized at various levels of aggregation by chemical stimuli, by hormonal and neural relations, by reproductive functions (mammalian mating rarely occurs without extrasexual or "reciprocal communication"), by learning specific adaptive functions, and finally, by filial, symbolic, economic, and consciously cooperative activities (whether they be ritually, mythically, or rationally expressed) — all of these are patently *not* coequal in form or content. To place a beehive, whose basic function is reproductive, and a town, whose basic function is cultural, under a common rubric, and then to merely distinguish them by their "degree" of complexity is not simply intellectually fatuous but ideologically insidious. Even the "socializing tendency" Kropotkin imputes to nature can be obfuscatory if it fails to recognize that institutions are never strictly or even primarily "natural," however much they seem to parallel fairly complex animal interactions. However prevalent mutual aid may be among nonhuman organisms, *social* cooperation presupposes will and intentionality, which is only dimly present in the animal world. By the same token, the widely touted "division of labor" which is falsely imputed to all kinds of animal communities, particularly the "social insects," is an *economic* fact — a specifically *human* one — not a variegated constellation of complementary functions and activities.

To ignore these distinctions is to invite considerable ideological mischief. Like the notions that nature is "cruel" or "kind," "stingy" or "generous," "harsh" or "gentle," we read back into levels of organic development behavioral criteria that have yet to be consolidated by human thought. Potentiality is not actuality, any more than tendency is the fruition of the possibilities it may yield. Society may be latent in nature, but it only comes into its truth as "true societies" (to use Wilson's jargon) through the cultural, economic, symbolic, and subjective interaction of organisms — and, let me emphasize, not by the mere presence of one or two of these traits but by the presence of *all* of them, woven into a common mosaic that is visibly and permanently organized. Social institutions may be rooted in consanguinity or in civil relations; they may be agrarian, with rich natural overtones, or urban, with strongly political ones — but in essence they are human because they are fabricated by disparate attributes, minimally conscious, communicative, and cooperatively economic ones. Bees and wasps are decidedly not "social" because their modes of organization, however elaborate and intricate, are massively predetermined by genetic codes. That is to say, they are rigidly fixed along uncreative, undevelopmental, and largely biochemical lines. That they actually form the genic "paradigm" for Wilson's concept of sociality is one of the most sinister features of sociobiology. Largely reproductive in function, the "social insects" represent the antithesis of any concept of evolution as untrammeled and emergent: they open no fresh or creative pathways in organic development but rather only an unswerving fixity and self-replication that from any innovative viewpoint represent a blind evolutionary alley.

In fact, a genetic strategy that makes the behavior of the "social insects" comprehensible actually renders human society incomprehensible. So-called primate "hierarchies" (a completely libelous term) yield strictly *individual* "dominance-submission" relationships (another libelous term) on the basis of largely physical attributes — notably, strength, hormonal fortitude, and possibly even intelligence, although the visible distinctions between a "smart" ape and a "dumb" one are barely noticeable in a primate community. It is quixotic ethologists like Jane Goodall-Lawick, rather than the apes themselves, who make these uniquely anthropomorphic distinctions. The myth of an intragroup "hierarchy" dissolves completely once we recognize that an "alpha" male chimpanzee is an individual creature, not an institution. His "dominant status" (whatever these words really mean) lives or dies with the fortunes of the ape, not with the fortunes of the group. Hence, "hierarchy" in the most "caste-like" apedoms or monkeydoms more closely resembles the links in a chain than layered and consciously empowered community structures.

This difference is a crucial one. A weak, enfeebled, unnerved, and sick ape is hardly likely to become an "alpha" male, much less retain this highly ephemeral "status." By contrast, the most physically and mentally pathological human rulers have exercised authority with devastating effect in the course of history and altered its destiny profoundly. The cry "The King is Dead! Long Live the King! " expresses a power of hierarchical *institutions* over persons that is completely reversed in so-called "animal hierarchies," where the absence of institutions is precisely the only intelligible way of talking about "alpha males" or "queen bees." Sociobiology, with its definitional reductionism, totally dissolves these crucial distinctions. "Hierarchy," to Wilson, is a "system of two or more levels of units, the higher level controlling at least to some extent the activities of the lower levels in order to integrate the group as a whole." One is tempted to observe that this "integrative" function must be hot news to an ape or a termite. In any case, the terms "system," "levels," "units," and "controlling" — so widely disparate throughout the animal world — are *precisely* the concepts and categories that Wilson is obliged to explain if the notion of "animal hierarchy" is to have meaning. These explanations are all the more necessary because "castes" of "worker bees" (another group of juicy terms) are in no way comparable to "alpha males" among primates. Wilson's fast-and-loose interchanging of "levels" and "units" allows him to recklessly pirouette around every part of animal ethology, from beehives to baboon troops. The genetic origins of beehive differentiation are blissfully transferred to less instinct-governed primate groups and then, almost joyously, to strictly contrived human social and political institutions.

From a definitional viewpoint, Wilson's terms and categories almost consistently beg the questions they are required to answer. A "caste" is "any set of individuals . . . that performs specialized labor in a colony." One is impelled to ask what "labor" means to Wilson in, say, a beehive, a wolf pack, a baboon troop, and a Detroit automobile factory. Can all of these "levels" of associations be flippantly subsumed under "labor"? And is "specialization" evidence of a "caste," a "profession," a "discipline," a "proclivity," a "calling," each guided by genetic, instinctive, psychological, economic, or creative sources? Or, after all, as Wilson would have it, are all of them reducible to the mere expression of "selfish genes" and an anthropomorphic myth of genic "morality"?

If one goes through most of Wilson's remaining socially charged definitions, sociobiology's landscape becomes increasingly depressing. Most seriously, Wilson's genic limits and biased definitions deny both nature and society's fecundity at best — or else dissolve them into the crassest form of social reactionism at worst. Wilson's genic "limits" to human behavior are not ideologically equivocal, as even some of his critics tend to believe. They are socially and politically reactionary. In *On Human Nature*, Wilson closes his tract with lyrical futuristic speculations that are inherently hostile to any emancipatory conception of human freedom. We learn that as sociobiology "enlarges" our knowledge of human nature, that we can erect our values on a more "objective basis," notably, a genetic one in which our "set of trajectories" or expectations, far from enlarging, "will narrow still more." Accordingly, Wilson, after having immersed us in a claw-and-fang social-Darwinism, in the very act of denying it rhetorically, opines that "we already know, to take two extreme examples, that the worlds of William Graham Summer, the absolute Social Darwinist, and Mikhail Bakunin, the anarchist, are biologically impossible. As the social sciences mature into predictive disciplines, the permissible trajectories will not only diminish in number but our descendants will be able to sight farther along them."

These remarks, which essentially foreclose any creative social flexibility beyond the specious limits of a chromosome. are evidence of totalitarian gall. They constitute a dogma of total surrender to social conditions as they are —social conditions, I would add, that are closer to social Darwinism today than in almost any period in humanity's bloody history. It is easy and rather superficial to criticize Wilson for his attempts to validate hierarchy, aggression, war, social domination, and conflict on biological grounds. These notions have been the flotsam-and-jetsam of sociology for decades. What renders Wilson's sociobiology particularly sinister is that it prostitutes the Hegelian notion (as vulgarized by Engels) that "freedom is the recognition of necessity" into a genic closure of all natural and social creativity. Wilson's "morality of the gene" is not only "selfish" but suffocatingly rigid; it not only impedes action with the autocracy of a genic tyrant, but closes the door to any action that is not biochemically defined by its own configuration. When freedom is nothing more than the recognition of necessity, when our expectations "narrow" as we discover the gene's tyranny over the greater totality of life, we are obliged to make the best of what we know we *cannot* do. *The possible becomes an expression of the impossible,* just as Wilson's notion of reason is interpreted as a mere "epiphenomenon" of neurology.

If sociobiology has anything to offer, it is a very harsh conclusion: when knowledge becomes dogma (and few movements are more dogmatic than sociobiology), freedom is ultimately denied. In Wilson's case, the freedom that is denied is not Summer's "absolute social-Darwinism" — for Summer's premises are built into sociobiology by definition, even as they are passingly rejected textually — but precisely the "extreme" which Wilson singles out from all others: the anarchism of a Mikhail Bakunin.

II

Our discussion of the reactionary content of sociobiology should not be permitted to conceal the problem it seeks to resolve. Biology, particularly in its relationship to society and ethics, has begun to acquire enormous, indeed highly controversial, importance. After a generation

60

in which these two topics have been ruthlessly dissociated from one another by academics, the issue of *objective* ethical criteria and society's interface with nature — an issue forced upon us by ecology — has made the need for a new continuum between them an imperative of programmatic importance. Our "place in nature," to use Max Scheler's phrase, is no longer to be evoked in wistfully romantic verbiage. It has become a philosophical challenge to overcome the dualism we inherited from Descartes and especially from Kant, the social scientism we inherited from Hobbes, the moral relativism we inherited from Hume, and the notion of a "blind," "mute" mechanical nature we inherited from Galileo.

Tragically, the need for meeting these challenges and resolving them is not forced by sociobiology alone, with its simplistic crudities. Like all sweeping issues of any historical period, the relationship of society and ethics to nature has been burdened by serious ideological tensions which have one-sidedly warped almost every intellectual contestant. Genic reductionism, in fact, is merely the coarsest weed in a larger bouquet whose constituents are only slightly less crude than sociobiology. It is unfortunate to note that a gifted evolutionary theorist like Stephen Jay Gould, for example, has reacted so sharply to the recent popularity of creationist theories of life that he denies any moral content to natural history. The temptation to react against one extreme, notably reborn Christianity, by evoking an equally questionable extreme like a mechanistic Darwinism, does no service to theories of biological evolution.

Mechanistic theories of evolution are as rooted in speculative prejudgments as creationism. By the same token, the shared failure of divine creationism and mechanistic evolutionism to resolve the moral and ecological problems created by our historic cleavage from nature has not been eliminated by infusing systems theory with a sovereign, all-encompassing importance — or worse, by surrounding it with a mystical halo borrowed from archaic, often quietistic Asian religious systems. The "California School of Mystics," if I may be permitted to so label writers like Fritjof Capra, Erich Jantsch, and for the hovering ghost of Gregory Bateson, is redolent of a systems theory as unspiritual and reductionist as the very mechanism it purports to oppose. The lavish quotations from Taoist and Buddhist literature do not alter the fact that systems theory is as mechanistic as the Newtonian image of the world as a clock. Feedback loops — whether negative or (in the case of Manfred Eigen and Ilya Prigogine) positive — are ultimately rooted in the mass-energy causalities and mathematical formulations that nourished Cartesian-Newtonian mechanisms. We should not permit our newly acquired aversion to a means-end" (or "linear") rationalism to cloak the fact that the "circular" rationalism of the California Mystics has simply replaced the clock with the radar set and the library with magnetic tapes. "Spaceship Earth" is still a spaceship, not a fecund, living planet that nourishes life.

Ultimately, it is not in oscillatory movements of feedback loops or an ill digested notion of form, "mentation," and "oneness" that a new ecological monism will be formulated. The recovery of the notion of "directiveness," which systems theory has brought to the foreground of natural and social evolution, is an advance of considerable importance. The natural world, in this light, can no longer be seen as "mute," nor can life and mind be viewed as the accidental epiphenomena of "blind" cosmic forces. "Nature," to use a highly abstract term, is fecund, not passive, and it consists of more than energy and mass (the traditional "matter" and "motion" mystique that orchestrated the crude materialism of the last century). By the same token, Teilhard de Chardin's "noosphere" is modern Neoplatonism writ large, and a Taoist "Oneness" that renders "God" as the "mind of the universe" (Jantsch) regresses to a religious archaism — and dualism — that classical Hellenic philosophy called *logos*.

Ludwig von Bertalanffy, who may well enjoy the distinction of being the most educated of the systems theorists, prudently distinguishes the most significant forms of directiveness or "dynamic teleology." There may be the simple direction of events to their final state or a purposive directiveness which Bertalanffy associates with Aristotle's notion of "final cause" or "equifinality," by which he means a given final state that can be reached in many different ways. Finally, Bertalanffy cites a directiveness "based on structure" which, carried beyond his own limited examples drawn from feedback mechanisms, suggests a concern with the nature of the nature of things. More than two millennia ago, Pythagoras emphasized more pointedly than his formalist (as distinguished from analytic) heirs — I refer here to systems theorists who have no substantial knowledge of the classical tradition — that it is as much in the nature of substance to direct itself toward form and complexity, to develop and grow — and with growth to achieve increasing subjectivity — as it is for matter to move. Neither oscillation alone nor accident, neither mass alone nor motion, but rather development and the self-organization of substance (all theological qualifications aside) constitute the innermost properties of being that render a natural *history*, an evolution of reality, possible. Hence a cosmic drama, it could be argued, does exist that is "directed" not by a deity exogenous to it or by a divine "architect" who fashions it; rather, it would be a *self*-directed and self-*unfolding* drama whose "finality" is as much an inherent property of substance as is motion. It is not simply by virtue of feedback loops and homeostatic mechanisms (the last is a well-chosen word) that substance would unfold self-directively, but rather by virtue of that delicious Aristotelian-Hegelian word "potentiality," the *entelechia* of phenomena, that would yield to the world particulars in their wholeness and fullness as a rich unity of diversity. Hence, "integration" and "oneness" would be reworded to convey the notion of a fecund pattern of interdependent phenomena, an ecosystem whose development comes from its uniqueness, not its homeostatic oscillations alone.

We would thus live in a world that is not lacking in meaning. Perhaps more significantly, such meaning as it had would be liberating in the sense that it would impart to human goals a purposiveness that brings a highly self-reflective nature — mentality itself — into the cosmos, freed from the confines of a purely privatistic and epistemological approach to ethics. We might say with Hans Jonas that this "Ontology as the ground of ethics was the original tenet of philosophy. Their divorce, which is the divorce of the 'objective' and 'subjective' realms, is the modern destiny. Their reunion can be effected, if at all, only from the 'objective' end, that is to say, through a revision of the idea of nature. And it is 'becoming' rather than 'abiding' nature that would hold out any such promise. From the immanent direction of its total evolution there could be elicited a destination of man by whose terms the person, in the act of fulfilling himself, would at the same time realize a concern of universal substance. Hence would result a principle of ethics which is ultimately grounded neither in the autonomy of the self nor in the needs of the community, but in an objective assignment by the nature of things."

What is most fascinating, however, is that "Nature" (*metaphorically* speaking) is writing its own nature philosophy and ethics — not the logicians, positivists, sociobiologists, mystics, and heirs of Galilean scientism. It is becoming increasingly evident that we are not "alone" in the universe, not even in the emptiness of space, as Bertrand Russell would have us believe. Owing to what is a fairly recent revolution in astrophysics (possibly comparable only to the achievements of Copernicus and Kepler), the cosmos is opening itself up to us in new ways that call for an exhilarating and speculative turn of mind and a more qualitative approach to natural phenomena. It is becoming increasingly tenable to suggest that the *entire* universe may be the cradle of life — not merely our own planet or planets like it. The "Big Bang," whose faint echoes from more than fifteen billion years ago can now be detected by the astrophysicist's instruments, may be evidence less of a single accidental event than of a form of cosmic "breathing" whose gradual expansions and contractions extend over an infinity of time. If this is so — and we are admittedly on highly speculative grounds — we may be dealing with cosmic processes rather than a single episode in the formation of the universe. Obviously, if these processes express an unending form of universal "history," as it were, we, who are irrevocably locked into our own cosmic era, may never be able to fathom their reality or meaning. But it is not completely unreasonable to wonder if we are dealing here with a vast, continuing development of the universe, not simply with a recurring type of cosmic "respiration."

Highly conjectural as these notions may be, the formation of all the elements from hydrogen and helium, their combination into small molecules and later into self-forming macromolecules, and finally the organization of these macromolecules into the constituents of life and possibly of mind follow a sequence that challenges Russell's image of humanity as an accidental spark in an empty, meaningless void. Certain phases of this sequence constitute a strong challenge to a view in which the word "accident" becomes a prudent substitute for virtual inevitabilities. A cosmos interspersed with dust composed of hydrogen, carbon, nitrogen, and oxygen molecules seems geared to the formation of organic molecules. Radio astronomers have detected cyanogen, carbon monoxide, hydrogen cyanide, formaldehyde, formic acid, methanol, acetaldehyde, and methyl formate in interstellar space. In short, the classical image of space as a void is giving way to the image of space as a restlessly active chemogenetic ground for an astonishing sequence of increasingly complex organic compounds.

From there, it is only a short leap to the self-organization of rudimentary life-forming molecules. Analysis of carbonaceous chondrites (a group of stony meteorites with small glassy inclusions) yields longchain aromatic hydrocarbons such as fatty acids, amino acids, and porphyrins — the compounds from which chlorophyll is built. In a series of laboratory studies beginning with the famous Miller-Urey "spark-gap" experiment, simple amino acids were formed by passing electrical discharges through a flask containing gases that presumably composed the earth's early atmosphere. By changing the gases in accordance with later theories of the primal atmosphere, other researchers have been able to produce long-chain amino acids, ribose and glucose sugars, and nucleoside phosphates — the precursors of DNA.

Hypothetically (albeit with an impressive degree of supporting evidence), it is now possible to trace how anaerobic microorganisms might have developed simple membranes and how, with increasing complexity, they have emerged as distinct life forms capable of highly developed metabolic processes. Few working hypotheses more strikingly reveal the highly graded interface between the inorganic and the organic than speculations on the formation of genetic structures. Such speculations bring us conceptually to the most central feature of life itself: the ability of a complex mosaic of organic macromolecules to reproduce itself and yet to do so with changes significant enough to render evolution possible. As early as 1944, Erwin Schrödinger may have provided a clue to organic reproduction and evolution. In *What is Life?* this eminent physicist observed that "the most essential part of a living cell — the chromosome fibre — may suitably be called an 'aperiodic crystal.'" The "chromosome fibre" does not merely repeat itself and grow additively, like a "periodic" crystal; instead, it changes significantly to yield new forms — mutations — that initiate and carry on inherited, evolutionary developments.

Graham Cairns-Smith has advanced another hypothesis (one among the many now being proposed and soon forthcoming) that may help clarify the nature of early reproductive processes. DNA is much too unstable chemically, Cairns-Smith emphasizes, to have survived the radiation and heat to which the early earth's surface was exposed. In an analogy that could bear improvement, Cairns-Smith compares DNA with a "magnetic tape: it is very efficient if provided with a suitably protective environment, suitably machined raw materials and suitably complex recording equipment." This machining equipment, he contends, can be found in the inorganic world itself:

> With a number of other considerations, this leads [Cairns-Smith] to the idea of a form of crystallization process as the printing machine, with some kind of crystal defects as the pattern-forming elements. Being as specific as possible, a mica-type clay seemed the most promising possibility.

Minimally, Cairns-Smith's hypothesis suggests that life, in its own ways and following its own genetic evolution, is not miraculously separated from phenomena existing in the inorganic world. I do not mean to imply that biology can be reduced to physics any more than society can be reduced to biology. Insofar as Cairns-Smith suggests that certain clay crystals could possibly be templates of organic reproductive material and thereby launch the evolution of secondary and still more advanced forms of organic hereditary materials, he is also suggesting that nature may be unified by certain common tendencies. Such tendencies would share a like origin in the reality of the cosmos, however differently they function at different levels of self-organization.

My point here is that substance and its properties are not separable from life. Henri Bergson's conception of the biosphere as an "entropy-reduction" factor, in a cosmos that is supposedly moving toward greater entropy or disorder, would seem to provide life with a cosmic rationale for existence. That life forms may have this function need not suggest that the universe has been exogenously "designed" by a supernatural demiurge. But it does suggest that "matter" or substance has inherent self-organizing properties, no less valid than the mass and motion attributed to it by Newtonian physics .

Nor is there so great a lack of data, by comparison with the conventional attributes of "matter," as to render the new properties implausible. At the very least, science must *be* what nature really is; and in nature, life *is* (to use Bergsonian terminology) a counteracting force to the second law of thermodynamies — or an "entropy-reduction" factor. The self-organization of substance into ever more complex forms — indeed, the importance of form itself as a correlate of function and of function as a correlate of self-organization — implies the unceasing activity to achieve stability. That stability as well as complexity is a "goal" of substance; that complexity, not only inertness, makes for stability; and finally, that complexity is a paramount feature of organic evolution and of an ecological interpretation of biotic interrelationships — all these concepts taken together are ways of understanding the natural world as such, not mere mystical vagaries. They are supported more by evidence than are the theoretical prejudices that still exist today against a universe charged with meaning.

This much is clear: we can no longer be satisfied with a passive "dead" matter that fortuitously collects into living substance. The universe bears witness to an ever-striving, *developing* — not merely a "moving" — substance, whose most dynamic and creative attribute is its ceaseless capacity for self-organization into increasingly complex forms. Natural fecundity originates primarily from growth, not from spatial "changes" of location. Nor can we remove form from its central place in this developmental and growth process, or function as an indispensable correlate of form. The orderly universe that makes science a possible project and its use of a highly concise logic — mathematics — meaningful presupposes the correlation of form with function. From this perspective, mathematics serves not merely as the "language" of science but also as the *logos* of science. This scientific *logos* is above all a workable project because it grasps a *logos* that inheres in nature — the "object" of scientific investigation.

Once we step beyond the threshold of a purely instrumental attitude toward the "language" of the sciences, we can admit even more attributes into our account of the organic substance we call life. Conceived as substance that is perpetually self-maintaining or metabolic as well as developmental, life more clearly establishes the existence of another attribute: symbiosis. Recent data support the view that Peter Kropotkin's mutualistic naturalism not only applies to relationships within and among species, but also applies morphologically — within and among complex cellular forms. As William Trager observed more than a decade ago:

> The conflict in nature between different kinds of organisms has been popularly expressed in phrases like "struggle for existence" and "survival of the fittest." Yet few people realize that mutual cooperation between different kinds of organisms — symbiosis — is just as important, and that the " fittest" may be the one that most helps another to survive.

Whether intentional or not, Trager's description of the "fittest" is not merely a scientific judgment made by an eminent biologist; it is also an ethical judgment similar to the one Kropotkin derived from his own work as a naturalist and his ideals as an anarchist. Trager emphasized that the "nearly perfect" integration of " symbiotic microorganisms into the economy of the host . . . has led to the hypothesis that certain intracellular organelles might have been originally independent microorganisms." Accordingly, the chloroplasts that are responsible for photosynthetic activity in plants with *eucaryotic,* or nucleated, cells are discrete structures that replicate by division, have their own distinctive DNA very similar to that of circular bacteria, synthesize their own proteins, and are bounded by two-unit membranes.

Much the same is true of the eucaryotic cell's "powerhouse," its mitochondria. The eucaryotic cells are the morphological units of all complex forms of animal and plant life. The protista and fungi also share these well-nucleated cell structures. Eucaryotes are aerobic and include clearly formed subunits, or organelles. By contrast, the *procaryotes* lack nuclei; they are anaerobic, less specialized than the eucaryotics, and they constitute the evolutionary predecessors of the eucaryotics. In fact, they are the only life forms that could have survived and flourished in the early earth's atmosphere, with its mere traces of free oxygen.

It is now widely accepted that the eucaryotic cells consist of highly functional symbiotic arrangements of procaryotes that have become totally interdependent with other constituents. Eucaryotic flagella derive from anaerobic spirochetes; mitochondria, from procaryotic bacteria that were capable of respiration as well as fermentation; and plant chloroplasts from "blue-green algae," which have recently been reclassified as cyanobacteria. The theory, now almost a biological convention, holds that *phagocytic* ancestors of what were to become eucaryotes absorbed (without digesting) certain *spirochetes*, protomitochondria, and, in the case of photosynthetic cells, *coccoid cyanobacteria* and *chloroxybacteria*. Existing phyla of multicellular aerobic life forms thus had their origins in a symbiotic process that integrated a variety of microorganisms into what can reasonably be called a colonial organism, the eucaryotic cell. *Mutualism*, not predation, seems to have been the guiding principle for the evolution of the highly complex aerobic life forms that are common today.

The prospect that life and all its attributes are *latent* in substance as such, that biological evolution is rooted deeply in symbiosis or mutualism, indicates how important it is to reconceptualize our notion of "matter" as *active* substance. As Manfred Eigen has put it, molecular self-organization suggests that evolution "appears to be an inevitable event, given the presence of certain matter with specified autocatalytic properties and under the maintenance of the finite (free) energy flow [that is, solar energy] necessary to compensate for the steady production of entropy." Indeed, this self-organizing activity extends beyond the emergence and evolution of life to the seemingly inorganic factors that produced and maintain a biotically favorable "environment" for the development of increasingly complex life forms. The traditional assumption that life has been forced merely to adapt to an independent, geologically and meteorologically determined "environment" is no longer tenable. This dualism between the living and the nonliving world (which is based on accidental point mutations in life-forms that determine what species will evolve or perish) is being replaced by the more challenging notion that life creates to a great degree its own environment on a worldwide scale.

Finally, the Modern Synthesis, to use Julian Huxley's term for the neo-Darwinian model of organic evolution in force since the early 1940s, has also been challenged as too narrow and perhaps mechanistic in its outlook. The image of a slow pace of evolutionary change emerging

68

from the interplay of small variations, which are selected for their adaptability to the environment, is no longer as supportable as it seemed by the actual facts of the fossil record. Evolution seems to be more sporadic, marked by occasional rapid changes, often delayed by long periods of stasis. Highly specialized genera tend to speciate and become extinct because of the very narrow, restricted niches they occupy ecologically, while fairly generalized genera change more slowly and become extinct less frequently because of the more diversified environments in which they can exist. This "Effect Hypothesis," advanced by Elizabeth Vrba, suggests that evolution tends to be an immanent striving rather than the product of external selective forces. Mutations appear more like intentional mosaics than small, scratch-like changes in the structure and function of life forms. As one observer notes, "Whereas species selection puts the forces of change on environmental conditions, the Effect Hypothesis looks to internal parameters that affect the rates of speciation and extinction."

The notion of small, gradual point mutations (a theory that accords with the Victorian mentality of strictly fortuitous evolutionary changes) can be challenged on genetic grounds alone. Not only a gene but a chromosome, both in varying combinations, may be altered chemically and mechanically. Genetic changes may range from "simple" point mutations, through jumping genes and transposable elements, to major chromosomal rearrangements. It is also clear, mainly from experimental work, that permutations of genetically determined *morphological* shifts are possible. Small genetic changes can give rise to either minor or major morphological modifications; the same holds true for large genetic changes.

Trager's observation that the "fittest" species may well be "the one that most helps another to survive" is an excellent formula for recasting the traditional picture of natural evolution as a meaningless competitive tableau bloodied by the struggle to survive. There is a rich literature, dating back to the late nineteenth century, that emphasizes the role played by intraspecific and interspecific symbiosis in fostering the survival of life forms on the planet. Kropotkin's famous *Mutual Aid* summarized the data at the turn of the century, and may have added the word "mutualism" to the biological vocabulary on symbiosis. Buchner has written a huge volume (1953) on the endosymbiosis of animals with plant microorganisms alone. Henry has compiled a two-volume work, *Symbiosis*, that brings the study of this subject up to the mid-1960s. The evidence for interspecific symbiosis, particularly mutualism, is nothing less than massive. Even more than Kropotkin's *Mutual Aid*, Henry's work traces the evidence of mutualistic relationships from the interspecific support relationships of rhizobia and legumes, through plant associations, behavioral symbiosis in animals, and the great regulatory mechanisms that account for homeostasis in planet-wide biogeochemical relationships.

"Fitness" is rarely biologically meaningful as mere species survival and adaptation. Left on this superficial level, it becomes an almost personal adaptive enterprise that fails to account for the need of all species for life support systems, be they autotrophic or heterotrophic. Traditional evolutionary theory tends to abstract a species from its ecosystem, to isolate it, and to deal with its survival in a remarkably abstract fashion. For example, the mutually supportive interplay between photosynthetic life forms and herbivores, far from providing evidence of the simplest form of "predation," or heterotrophy, is in fact indispensable to soil fertility from animal wastes, seed distribution, and the return (via death) of bulky organisms to an ever-enriched ecosystem. Even large carnivores that prey upon large herbivores have a vital function in selectively controlling large population swings by removing weakened or old animals for whom life would in fact become a form of "suffering."

Ironically, it cheapens the meaning of the real *suffering* and *cruelty* inflicted by *society*, reducing them to pain and predation, just as it cheapens the meaning of hierarchy and domination, to deinstitutionalize these socially charged terms and dissolve them into the individual transitory links between more or less aggressive individuals within a specific animal aggregation. The fear, pain, and commonly rapid death that a wolfpack brings to a sick or old caribou are evidence not of suffering or cruelty in nature but of a mode of dying that is integrally wedded to organic renewal and ecological stability. Suffering and cruelty properly belong to the realm of personal anguish, needless affliction, and the moral degradation of those who torment the victim. These notions cannot be applied to the removal of an organism that can no longer function on a level that renders its life tolerable. It is sheer distortion to associate all pain with suffering, all predation with cruelty. To suffer the anguish of hunger, psychic injury, insecurity, neglect, loneliness, and death in warfare, as well as of prolonged trauma and terminal illness, cannot be equated with the pain associated with predation and the unknowing fact of death. The spasms of the natural world are rarely as cruel as the highly organized and systematic afflictions that human society visits upon healthy, vital beings — animal as well as human — afflictions that only the cunning of the hominid mind can contrive.

70

Neither cruelty, aggression, nor competition — all anthropomorphic terms — satisfactorily explains the emergence and evolution of life. For a better explanation we should also turn to mutualism and a concept of "fitness" that reinforces the support systems for the seemingly "fittest." If we are prepared to recognize the self-organizing nature of life, the decisive role of mutualism as its evolutionary impetus obliges us to redefine "fitness" in terms of an ecosystem's supportive apparatus. And if we are prepared to view life as a phenomenon that can shape and maintain the very "environment" that is regarded as the "selective" source of its evolution, a crucial question arises: Is it meaningful any longer to speak of "natural selection" as the motive force of biological evolution? Or must we now speak of "natural interaction" to take full account of life's own role in creating and guiding the "forces" that explain its evolution? Contemporary biology leaves us with a picture of organic interdependencies that far and away prove to be more important in shaping life forms than a Darwin, a Huxley, or the formulators of the Modern Synthesis could ever have anticipated. Life is necessary not only for its own self-maintenance but also for its own self-formation. Complexity and subjectivity are more than the effects of life; they are its integral attributes.

The grandeur of an authentic ecological sensibility, in contrast to the superficial environmentalism so prevalent today, is that it provides us with the ability to generalize in the most radical way these fecund, supportive interrelationships and their reliance on variety as the foundation of stability. An ecological sensibility gives us a coherent outlook that is explanatory in the most meaningful sense of the term, and almost overtly *ethical*.

From the distant Hellenic era to the early Renaissance, nature was seen primarily as a source of ethical orientation, a means by which human thought found its normative bearings and coherence. Nonhuman nature was not external to human nature and society. To the contrary, the mind was uniquely part of a cosmic *logos* that provided objective criteria for social and personal concepts of good and evil, justice and injustice, beauty and ugliness, love and hatred — indeed, for an interminable number of values by which to guide oneself toward the achievement of virtue and the good life. The words *dike* and *andike* — justice and injustice — permeated the cosmologies of the Greek nature philosophers. They linger on in many terminological variations as part of the jargon of modern natural science — notably as "attraction" and "repulsion."

The principal fallacies of archaic cosmology generally lie not in its ethical orientation but in its dualistic approach to nature. For all its emphasis on speculation at the expense of experimentation, ancient cosmology erred most when it tried to co-join a self-organizing, fecund nature with a vitalizing force alien to the natural world itself. Parmenides's Dike, like Henri Bergson's *élan vital*, are substitutes for the self-organizing properties of nature, not motivating forces within nature that account for an ordered world. A latent dualism exists in monistic cosmologies that try to bring humanity and nature into ethical commonality — a *deus ex machina* that corrects imbalances either in a disequilibriated cosmos or in an irrational society. Truth wears an unseen crown in the form of God or Spirit, for nature can never be trusted to develop on its own spontaneous grounds, any more than the body politic bequeathed to us by "civilization" can be trusted to manage its own affairs.

These archaisms, with their theological nuances and their tightly formulated teleologies, have been justly viewed as socially reactionary traps. In fact, they tainted the works of Aristotle and Hegel as surely as they mesmerized the minds of the medieval Schoolmen. But the errors of classical nature philosophy lie not in its project of eliciting an ethics from the natural world, but in the spirit of domination that poisoned it from the start with a presiding, often authoritarian, Supernatural "arbiter" who weighed out and corrected the imbalances or "injustices" that erupted in nature. Hence the dark ancient gods were there all the time, however rationalistic these early cosmologies may seem; they had to be exorcised in order to render an ethical continuum between the natural world and humanity more meaningful. Tragically, late Renaissance thought was hardly more evolutionary than its antecedents, and neither Galileo in science nor Descartes in philosophy performed this much-needed act of surgery satisfactorily. They and their more recent heirs *separated* the domains of nature and mind, recreating deities of their own in the form of scientistic and epistemological biases that are no less tainted by domination than the classical tradition they demolished.

Today, we are faced with the possibility of permitting natural evolution—not Dike, Justitia, God, Spirit, or an *élan vital*—to open itself to us for ethical purposes on its *own* terms. Mutualism is a good by virtue of its function in fostering the evolution of natural variety. We require no Dike on the one hand or canons of "scientific objectivity" on the other to affirm the role of community as a desideratum in nature and society. Similarly, *freedom* is a good; its claims are validated by what Hans Jonas so perceptively called the "inwardness" of life forms, their "organic identity" and "adventure of form." The clearly visible effort, venture, indeed self-recognition, which every living being exercises in the course of "its precarious metabolic continuity" to preserve itself reveals—even in the most rudimentary of organisms—a sense of identity and selective activity which Jonas has very appropriately called evidence of "germinal freedom."

Finally, from the ever-greater complexity and variety that raises subatomic particles through the course of evolution to those conscious, self-reflexive life forms we call human beings, we cannot help but speculate about the existence of a broadly and latent subjectivity in substance itself that eventually yields mind and intellectuality. In the reactivity of substance, in the sensibility of the least-developed microorganisms, in the elaboration of nerves, ganglia, the spinal cord, and the layered development of the brain, one senses an evolution of mind so coherent and compelling that there is a strong temptation to describe it with Manfred Eigen's term, "inevitable." It is hard to believe that mere fortuity accounts for the capacity of life forms to respond neurologically to stimuli; to develop highly organized nervous systems; to be able to foresee, however dimly, the results of their behavior and later conceptualize this foresight clearly and symbolically. A true history of mind may have to begin with the attributes of substance itself; perhaps in the hidden or covert efforts of the simplest crystals to perpetuate themselves, in the evolution of DNA from unknown chemical sources to a point where it shares a principle of replication already present in the inorganic world, and in the speciation of nonliving as well as living molecules as a result of those intrinsic self-organizing features of reality we call their "properties."

Hence our study of nature—all archaic philosophies and epistemological biases aside—exhibits a self-evolving patterning, a "grain," so to speak, that is implicitly ethical. Mutualism, freedom, and subjectivity are not strictly human values or concerns. They appear, however *germinally,* in larger cosmic and organic processes that require no Aristotelian God to motivate them, no Hegelian Spirit to vitalize them. If social ecology provides little more than a coherent focus to the unity of mutualism, freedom, and subjectivity as aspects of a cooperative society that is free of domination and guided by reflection and reason, it will remove the taints that blemished a naturalistic ethics from its inception; it will provide both humanity and a natural world with a common ethical voice. No longer would we have need of a Cartesian— and more recently, a neo-Kantian—dualism that leaves the natural world mute and mind isolated from the larger world of phenomena around it. To vitiate community, to arrest the spontaneity that lies at the core of a self-organizing reality toward ever greater complexity and rationality, to abridge freedom — these actions would cut across the grain of natural evolution, deny our heritage in its evolutionary processes, and dissolve our legitimacy and function in the world of life. No less than this ethically rooted legitimation is at stake — all its grim ecological consequences aside — in achieving an ecological society and articulating an ecological ethics.

Mutualism, self-organization, freedom, and subjectivity, together with social ecology's principles of unity in diversity, informed spontaneity, and non-hierarchical relationships, coheers into an ethics of complementarity that sees human beings in a rational, ecological society as playing the creative role of "nature" rendered self-conscious. Aside from the ecological responsibilities this ethics confers on our species as the self-reflexive voice of nature, it literally defines us. "Nature," conceived *as* natural evolution, does not "exist" for us to use; it *legitimates* us and *our uniqueness* ecologically. Like the concept of "being," these principles of social ecology require no explanation, merely verification. They are the elements of an ethical *ontology*, not "rules of a game" that can be changed to suit one's personal needs.

A society that cuts across the grain of this ethical ontology raises the entire question of its very reality as a meaningful and rational entity. "Civilization" has bequeathed us a vision of otherness as "polarization" and "defiance," and of organic "inwardness" as a perpetual "war" for self-identity. Whatever its validity in the past, this vision now threatens to utterly subvert the ecological legitimation of humanity and the reality of society as a potentially rational dimension of the world around us. Trapped by the perception of a "Nature" that stands in perpetual opposition to our humanity, we have redefined humanity itself to mean strife as a condition for harmony, control as a condition for consciousness, domination as a condition for freedom, and opposition as a condition for reconciliation.

Yet an entirely different ethical, philosophical, and social dispensation can be read from the concept of otherness and the inwardness of life. Given a world that life itself made conducive to evolution — indeed, benign, in view of a larger ecological vision of "Nature" — we can formulate an ethics of complementarity that is nourished by variety and a creative participation in the natural world guided by reason and empathy, rather than one that guards individual inwardness from a threatening, hostile, invasive otherness. Indeed, the inwardness of life can be seen as an expression of mutualism, not as mere resistance to entropy and the terminus of all activity. Entropy itself can be seen as one feature in a larger cosmic metabolism, with life as its anabolic dimen-

74

sion. Finally, self hood can be viewed as the result of integration, community, support, and sharing without any loss of individual identity and personal spontaneity.

Civilization as we know it *today* is more mute than the nature for which it professes to speak and more blind than the elemental forces it professes to control. Indeed, civilization today lives in hatred of the world around it and in grim hatred of itself. Its gutted cities, wasted lands, poisoned air and water, and mean-spirited greed constitute a daily indictment of its odious immorality. A world so demeaned may well be beyond redemption, at least within the terms of its own institutional and ethical framework. The thermonuclear flames and the ecological disasters that may engulf our planet will render it irretrievably inhospitable to life — a dead witness to cosmic failure. If only because this planet's history, including its human history, has been so full of promise, hope, and creativity, it deserves a better fate than what seems to confront it in the years ahead.

Some Recent Titles from AK Press

BAD by James Carr, introduction by Dan Hammer; ISBN 1 873176 21 X; 224 pp two color cover, perfect bound 6 x 9; £5.95/$7.95. "When I was 9 years old, I burned down my school." So begins the searing autobiography of a former child prodigy of crime in the streets of LA's ghettos. He relates the story of his life with cold passion, illuminating the daily life on the streets and in prison. First published and banned in 1975. This is its first reprinting.

TESTCARD F: TELEVISION, MYTHINFORMATION AND SOCIAL CONTROL constructed by Anonymous; ISBN 1 873176 91 0; 80 pp four color cover, perfect bound 5-1/2 x 8-1/2; £4.50/$6.00. Using savage image-text cut and paste, this book explodes all previous media theory and riots through the Global Village, looting the ideological supermarket of all its products.

END TIME: NOTES ON THE APOCALYPSE by G.A. Matiasz; ISBN 1873176 96 1; 320 pp four color cover, perfect bound 5-1/2 x 8-1/2; £5.95/$7.00. A first novel by G.A. Matiasz, an original voice of slashing, thought provoking style. "A compulsively readable thriller combined with a very smart meditation on the near-future of anarchism, *End Time* proves once again that science fiction is our only literature of ideas." — Hakim Bey

NO PITY by Stewart Home; ISBN 1 873176 46 5; 144 pp two color cover, perfect bound 5-1/2 x 8-1/2; £7.50/$12.95. With this collection of nine short stories, Mr. Home gives fiction back the bad name it deserves.

STEALWORKS: THE GRAPHIC DETAILS OF JOHN YATES by John Yates; ISBN 1 873176 51 1; 136 pp two color cover, perfect bound 8-1/2 x 11; £7.95/$11.95. A collection to date of work created by a visual mechanic and graphic surgeon. His work is a mixture of bold visuals, minimalist to-the-point social commentary, involves the manipulation and reinterpretation of culture's media imagery.

ECSTATIC INCISIONS: THE COLLAGES OF FREDDIE BAER by Freddie Baer, preface by Peter Lamborn Wilson; ISBN 1 873176 60 0; 80 pages, a three color cover, perfect bound 8-1/2 x 11; £7.95/$11.95. This is Freddie Baer's first collection of collage work. Includes collaborations with Hakim Bey, T. Fulano, Jason Keehn, and David Watson.

AK Press publishes and distributes a wide variety of radical literature. For our latest catalog featuring these and several thousand other titles, please send a large self-addressed, stamped envelope to:

AK Press
22 Lutton Place
Edinburgh, Scotland
8HE 9PE, Great Britain

AK Press
P.O. Box 40682
San Francisco, CA
94140-0682